101

CROSSWORDS

D1370760

Publications International, Ltd.

Puzzle creators: Deb Amlen, Sam Bellotto Jr., Patrick Blindauer, Myles Callum, Kelly Clark, Mark Danna, Gayle Dean, Harvey Estes, Ray Hamel, William I. Johnston, Matt Jones, Roy Leban, Alan Olschwang, Fred Piscop, Brendan Quigly, Nancy Salomon, Terry Stickels, Ben Tausig, Wayne Robert Williams

Puzzle illustrators: Helem An, Chris Gattorna, Elizabeth Gerber, Robin Humer, Shavan R. Spears, Jen Torche

Louis Weber, CEO
Publications International, Ltd.
8140 Lehigh Avenue
Morton Grove, IL 60053

Permission is never granted for commercial purposes.

ISBN: 978-1-68022-891-5

Manufactured in China.

8 7 6 5 4 3 2 1

Crossword puzzles are a true test of your pop-culture and general-trivia knowledge, and *Brain Games®: 101 Crosswords* is perfect for testing that knowledge wherever you're going. Page after page, it will challenge you to creatively deduce the answers from its allusive clues. Like pieces of a puzzle, each answer correlates with the others that surround it, adding bits of information to unsolved clues to help you make lateral and longitudinal progress. What is a three-letter word for a modern ID verifier? What 1987 Diane Keaton movie has eight letters in its title? What is a four-letter word for an Abu Dhabi denizen? What is a denizen, anyways? Use the answers you already know to guide you toward solving more obscure sections of the puzzle. Shuffle through the pages of your most trusted dictionary, thesaurus, atlas, quotation resource, and almanac for a helping hand, and you will most definitely begin to work your way through the challenges of *Brain Games®: 101 Crosswords*.

The puzzles may be difficult, but there are many ways in which you can solve these trivial challenges. First of all, always work in pencil, because you never know when an answer you're "pretty" sure about ends up not fitting into the greater scheme of the puzzle. Also, always try to solve the fill-in-the-blank clues first; they are generally an easy access point into the more difficult sections of the puzzle. Other tips that may get your momentum going include trying to solve two- and three-letter, plural, and abbreviated clues first. These will hint at some of the longer, more difficult clues that you have not yet tackled. If none of this works, and you can't for the life of you figure out what a seven-letter word for "Is unable to grasp, as a point" is, there is always an answer key in the back of the book to help you. *Brain Games®: 101 Crosswords* is filled with trivial variety and intellectual hurdles that will captivate you even during the most lackluster parts of your day.

QUESTIONABLE TUNES

ACROSS

1. Map collection
6. "Mamma Mia!" band
10. Mop's companion
14. Mail carrier's itinerary
15. Handyman's need
16. Island near Corsica
17. Marvin Gaye song of 1963
20. "Hurry up!"
21. Atlanta ball team
22. Dirt Devil, for short
23. "Tonight Show" host
24. Newswoman Katie
28. Weeps with abandon
29. Calf catcher
30. With 38-ACROSS, Tom Jones' song of 1965
35. Cry of dismay
36. Denzel's "_____ on Fire"
37. Sweep under the rug
38. See 30-ACROSS
41. Preserved, in a way
43. Letters of debt
44. New York City borough
45. Begin or Sharon
49. Astronaut Grissom
50. Verdi opera
51. "Obey me!"
56. Beach Boys song of 1962
58. Big name in dog food
59. A pop
60. Actress Luft
61. Abode for a bird
62. Commits perjury
63. Snide expression

DOWN

1. Rainbow paths
2. Exactly
3. Half-moon shape
4. Restaurant requisite
5. Classical guitar great
6. Room at the top
7. Fishing vessel
8. Gift decoration
9. Fictional password user
10. Prison-related
11. Motrin competitor
12. "A Doll's House" playwright
13. Capture, in a way
18. Pass a bill
19. Meeting for lovers
23. Sportscaster Madden
24. Shoe sound
25. Pearl Harbor locale
26. Coffee dispensers
27. Mexican rivers
28. Hits flies
31. Cobbler's creation
32. Reebok competitor
33. Biblical garden
34. Joins in holy matrimony
36. Hawaiian island
39. Triangular road sign
40. K.F.C. founder, with "the"
41. Young pigeon
42. Seafood in shells
45. Des Moines resident
46. Went to second base, perhaps
47. Extends one's enlistment

48. Dispense in shares
49. Rome invaders
51. Rolled cubes
52. Get _____ a good thing

53. Address for a king
54. Teen woe
55. January through December
57. _____ chi

Answers on page 236.

ACROSS

1. Historic spans
5. Harbor city
9. Tour of duty
14. Soybean dish
15. Cookie often eaten inside-out
16. Creek transport
17. Underground worker
19. Hunter's weapon
20. Underwear maker
22. "Skedaddle!"
23. Remote control batteries
24. Crazy
28. George's role on "Cheers"
30. Ending with spy or web
33. Look for riches in a stream
35. Therefore, to Descartes
36. Embellish
37. Santa _____, CA
38. Parade attraction
39. Wolfe of fiction
40. Quick wash
42. Murals and such
43. Head honcho
44. Comes to
45. "Mel's Diner" waitress
46. Dr. of rap
47. Houston school
55. Put on cloud nine
56. NASCAR qualifier
58. Toll roads
59. Blood may do it
60. Spanish cooking pot
61. Full of pits

62. Egg producers
63. Scholarship criterion

DOWN

1. And so forth
2. Santa's landing spot
3. Many miles away
4. "Star Trek" navigator
5. Actor Sidney
6. "Believe it _____!"
7. Atoll protector
8. Legal wrong
9. Haunted house reaction
10. Coin toss option
11. The lowdown, for short
12. _____ contendere (defendant's plea)
13. Swarm (with)
18. Filet follower
21. Like a rock
24. Bucky Beaver's toothpaste
25. Consumer watchdog Ralph
26. Sound of contempt
27. Curly coif
28. Desserts, to many dieters
29. _____ Mills photography studios
30. Frog sound
31. Stone with curved, colored bands
32. Closet pests
34. Spaces between teeth
35. Where Napoleon was exiled
38. Least in amount
40. Any day now
41. Attics for artists

43. Like Billie Holiday songs
45. Honored with a big bash
46. Exorcism target
47. What weightlifters count
48. "Would _____ to you?"
49. Word that can follow the first word of 20-, 33-, 40-, and 47-ACROSS
50. Scratch target
51. Despicable
52. It may be cast or wrought
53. One of 100 in Scrabble
54. Harvard rival
57. Young chap

WATER YA EXPECT

ACROSS

1. Dire sign
5. Destination for a coin
9. On the ocean or in a fog
14. Artist Salvador
15. Leslie Caron musical
16. Coarse wool fabric
17. Part of CEO
18. Shopping list addition
19. Watch sounds
20. "Stand By Me" actor
23. Taunt
24. Kind of pen
28. Like a basset hound's ears
31. Film director Kazan
32. Yoko _____
33. Spine-chilling
34. Container for Jack and Jill
35. Fly without a co-pilot
36. Remote control button
39. LeBron's nickname
40. Produces eggs
41. Easily duped
42. Fraction of a joule
43. Poet St. Vincent Millay
44. Back against a wall
45. Like some eyes
47. Event for bargain hunters
48. Coat used as a restraint
53. Largest city in Nebraska
56. Prefix meaning "peculiar"
57. All-night bash
58. Sired, biblically
59. Carter of "Gimme a Break"
60. Ken or Lena of Hollywood
61. Very impressed
62. Stuff to the gills
63. Whip mark

DOWN

1. River dividing Germany and Poland
2. Shin-covering skirt
3. Mountain road sign abbr.
4. "Well done!"
5. Pass unnoticed
6. Like a ballerina's body
7. Breakfast spread
8. "The minutes zip by!"
9. King of the Huns
10. Between, poetically
11. Blink of an eye: abbr.
12. Comics cry
13. Annoying pop-ups
21. Become ready to pick
22. "Jurassic Park" actor Sam
25. "Yer dern _____!"
26. Under Cupid's spell
27. More destitute
28. Knocked down
29. Employ again
30. Juice source
31. Class that doesn't require much studying
34. Bananas' cousins
35. Straw man
37. Church leader
38. WWII bomber _____ Gay
43. Heirs split it
44. Persuade with promises
46. Expression of disbelief

47. Clown's prop
49. Bright thought
50. Curly-leafed veggie
51. Villainous

52. Campfire sight
53. Geisha's sash
54. Restroom sign
55. Turkish title of honor

1	2	3	4		5	6	7	8		9	10	11	12	13
14					15					16				
17					18					19				
20				21					22					
			23					24				25	26	27
28	29	30					31					32		
33						34					35			
36				37					38					
39				40					41					
42				43				44						
45			46				47							
		48				49					50	51	52	
53	54	55			56					57				
58					59					60				
61					62					63				

Answers on page 236.

MISH-MASH

ACROSS

1. Italian fried egg dish
9. Organizer Lech of Poland
15. Famous
16. What a flamingo often stands on
17. Shot from a barista
18. Like llamas
19. Ogle
20. College URL component
21. Actor Gulager
22. Removed the insides of
23. Little tyke
25. Swimmer Biondi, actor Damon
27. Tiny soldier
28. Asset of fresh celery
31. TV role for Bamboo Harvester
32. Have trouble believing
33. Stand against
35. Kind of hymn
38. Trattoria tipple
39. Hold opinion
40. Person, place, etc . . .
41. Sign of trouble
42. Conniver's concoction
44. Chem. class location, at times
47. Decaf brand
49. Camera type: abbr.
50. Without delay
52. RR terminal
53. Hoops org.
55. Whim
57. One under par
59. Spill preventer at the kiddie table
60. "Relax, soldiers"
61. Repair person's kit
62. Collection of literature excerpts
63. How bananas are bought

DOWN

1. Sprite rival
2. Lie atop
3. Not wholly
4. Dodger manager Joe
5. Stereotypical professorial garb
6. Looped handle
7. Science glassware
8. Furor
9. Blue dye worn by early Brits
10. Per _____
11. Showed the way
12. Negative particle
13. Old ice cream brand
14. Mass prayer
20. Yadda yadda yadda: abbr.
24. Ottawa's prov.
26. Oscars org.
29. Reigns
30. Bor-r-r-ring
32. Tipsy
34. Topping on Hawaiian pizza
35. Part of a bicycle frame
36. Iron ore
37. Undeveloped region
38. Duress

40. Stanley Cup awarder: abbr.
43. Union-opposing grp.
44. Secular
45. Point the finger at
46. Paged, in a way
48. Liqueur flavoring
51. Tony Award winner Jonathan

of "Miss Saigon"
54. "Duff," to Homer Simpson
56. Each
58. Ravi Shankar, to Norah Jones, informally
59. Actor Townsend, casually

Answers on page 236.

IT'S GOOD TO BE THE QUEEN

ACROSS

1. Singer whose life was made into a 1980 hit play
5. Bankrupt
9. "Suzie Q" band, for short
12. Like JFK Airport: abbr.
13. Brother of Jacob
14. Norma _____ (Sally Field role)
15. Screen queen of 1998
18. Barber's obstruction
19. Actor Christian
20. Balaam's mount
22. Tiny terror
25. *Año nuevo* time
26. Screen queen of 1955
29. Part of a Girl Scout's uniform
30. Mauna _____
31. It's across the Thames from Windsor Castle
35. Screen queen of 2009
38. "Sex and the City" drink
41. Bowman's need
42. Kabuki alternative
43. Aruba or Cuba
45. First name in dictators
47. Screen queen of 1971
52. Lend a hand
53. 1910 Rodin sculpture at the Met
54. Running shoe name
55. Hosp. employees
56. Sources of beta carotene
57. "And so on," when tripled

DOWN

1. Paparazzo's prize
2. "All _____ day's work"
3. Bears witness
4. Dog's bane
5. Seminary subj.
6. "Born in the _____"
7. Sirs Holm and McKellen
8. Cores
9. Home of the Minotaur
10. Provide nosh for, as a party
11. Fashionably nostalgic
16. Camembert kin
17. Brother in a fairy tale
20. Bodybuilder's pride
21. Poseidon's realm
23. 1551, in monuments
24. Saint in Italy
27. Authority figure, slangily
28. _____ *con Dios* (Spanish farewell)
32. Former French protectorate
33. Lennon's bride
34. Math degree?
36. When repeated, a Mamas and the Papas hit
37. _____-a-brac
38. Prop for George Burns
39. K.T. of country music
40. Seasonal transports
44. Arp art
46. Fashion inits.
48. Preserves
49. Morning hrs.
50. Initialed
51. PBS-supporting org.

Answers on page 236.

CLOTHING ALTERATIONS

ACROSS

1. Table extender
5. Midwest clock setting: abbr.
8. Fencer's sword
12. "My Name Is _____" (TV show)
13. _____ glance
14. Coffee bar containers
15. "*Cogito,* _____ *sum*" (Descartes)
16. Swiss-based relief group
18. Mexican treat for athletes?
20. Response to a captain
21. Generate
25. Sound from a terrier
28. Permission slip
31. Follow without question
32. Small imperfections in a dance?
35. Chin-stroking phrase
36. Scotch partner
37. Just manage, with "out"
38. Larceny, e.g.
40. "And so on": abbr.
42. Inventory gardening equipment?
48. Mexican musician
51. "_____ *con dias*"
52. Austin Powers player Myers
53. Middle of a kids' game
54. Next-to-last fairy tale word
55. Greek feeling of love
56. Bother
57. Comedian Foxx

DOWN

1. Brand of jeans
2. Tombstone's Wyatt
3. Jason's ship in Greek mythology
4. Botanical gardens display
5. Children ride in them
6. "Leave as is," editorially
7. "Presto!"
8. Music of Kylie Minogue or Roxette
9. For
10. USN rank
11. Letter before Tee
17. IV amts.
19. Key in
22. "_____ to leap tall buildings in a single bound"
23. Seven days in May, e.g.
24. Wall Street letters
25. "This won't hurt _____!"
26. Devil-may-care
27. Run away
29. One resident abode
30. Robin, to Batman
33. Southpaws
34. Well-traveled passage
39. Carol syllable
41. _____ Girl
43. Show opening
44. Blacken on the grill
45. Put in the bank
46. Black _____ Peas
47. Reddish-brown gem
48. Mrs., in France

49. _____ ball (terrible basketball shot)

50. Studio that released "Citizen Kane"

SNAKE PREVIEW

ACROSS

1. Smell awful
6. High wind
10. Watering holes
14. Tom's "Roseanne" role
15. Not much
16. River to the Caspian Sea
17. Stocking holder-upper
19. Place to wait
20. Roll-call call
21. "The Hustler" game
22. Accuse without proof
24. "Follow me!", colloquially
25. Your house, e.g.
26. Expired, as a subscription
29. Plain writing
32. Burglary deterrent
33. It has "*E pluribus unum*" on it
37. Stage after larva
38. Newspapers, magazines, etc.
39. Telemarketer's aim
40. Two-bit
42. Beast on an old nickel, really
43. Hearty enjoyment
44. Muffed in the infield
45. Haunted house sound
48. Dot on a map
49. Place of rapid growth
51. Potting need
52. Herbal drink
55. Israel airline
56. Jalopy
59. Nobelist Wiesel
60. Number for one
61. Shake awake

62. Inside-the-Beltway figures
63. 2005 Beck hit
64. "Trusty" horse

DOWN

1. "Iliad," e.g.
2. Waiter's tool
3. Regarding, on a memo
4. Annual b-ball tournament
5. "Don't say a word!"
6. French-speaking African nation
7. Genesis casualty
8. Rapper _____ Wayne
9. Songbird James
10. Informal discussion
11. First zodiac sign
12. Place to hit a bucket of balls
13. Winter road hazard
18. Cheer
23. Hang in there
24. City on Biscayne Bay
26. Speaks ill of
27. Reunion attendee
28. California wine county
29. First-class
30. Artist Magritte
31. Granola tidbit
33. John Wayne's "True _____"
34. All-star game side
35. Natural soother
36. What usurers do
38. Carat divs.
41. Gospel writer
42. When they strike, it's a good thing

44. Be angry as heck
45. Sound from the birdhouse
46. The rich kid in "Nancy"
47. Amazon.com business
48. Completely wreck
50. Race on Main Street, maybe
51. Use a swizzle stick

52. In alignment
53. Move carefully
54. Mimicked
57. Former Press Secretary Fleischer
58. Pre-K enrollee

Answers on page 237.

SPARE TIME

ACROSS

1. Beast of burden
4. Papua New Guinea city
7. Extinguishes
14. Rapper-turned-actor
16. Get rid of
17. What escapes
18. Beard-busting brand
19. Total bull
21. Israeli weapon
22. Charges
23. Treated, at dinner
27. Celestial Seasonings selections
29. Robot add-on
30. Intimidate, with "out"
31. Auburn hair dye
34. Free-for-alls
35. Murano specialty
38. Comb-over alternative
39. Lingo
40. Gets through easily
41. Broke bread
42. Like a 911 call: abbr.
46. Pins and needles are in it
47. Begs
50. "Wheel of Fortune" buy
51. Plasma product, often
54. "Fear Street" author: abbr.
57. "I'd wager…"
58. Party feeder
59. Friday's series
60. Lines at the Post Office?
61. Dusk, to Donne
62. Two-time loser to DDE: inits.

DOWN

1. Nearly
2. Smut
3. Justice Antonin _____
4. Sits around
5. Aquarium problem
6. Bouncer's activity
7. Black-and-white bamboo chewers
8. Horseshoe-shaped fastener
9. Spelling in pictures
10. Doesn't give up on a dream?
11. Crude business
12. The Trojans' school: abbr.
13. Howe'er
15. Gave one's blessing to
20. Snowballs
24. 43-DOWN's opposite: Span.
25. "Law & Order: SVU" co-star
26. Batters in the AL, but not the NL
28. One with hot stuff?
30. Dominican dough
32. Wool coat wearers
33. The way to San Jose, from Santa Cruz: abbr.
34. Much-maligned additive: abbr.
35. Give the _____
36. Doozy
37. 773, e.g.
38. It's past due: Ital.
41. Transforms
43. "*Hasta* _____"
44. Main menu choice

45. Captures, in a way
47. Window shopper's buys?
48. Big name in hip-hop
49. Family car
52. Pre-euro money in Italy

53. Oft-sampled South Bronx band
54. Record co. name
55. Schoolboy
56. Normal: abbr.

IN CORPORO SANO

ACROSS

1. Utmost degree
4. Jamaica, the Bahamas, etc.: abbr.
7. Pierce
11. City on the Tigris
13. "The _____ of the Screw"
14. Ripped
15. Pine juice
16. "Tell it like _____"
17. Russian mountains
18. Precedes
20. Little hill
21. Avoiding the issue
23. Mr.'s companion
24. Costello
25. Forbid
28. Mediterranean island nation
32. Paint a word picture
34. Arctic or Indian
35. Little one
36. New York state creeks
37. Dangerous place to be
39. Finger _____
40. Begley and Asner
41. Curse
42. Simian
44. Dangerous part of the road
50. Soak
53. Hint at
54. Modern Persia
55. Jai _____
56. Robby Burns's "don't"
57. Mexican money
58. Sea bird
59. To be: Sp.
60. Prophet
61. Chemical suffix
62. "Norma _____"

DOWN

1. Cartoonist Thomas and family
2. Attempts
3. Male place to buy tools
4. Hawk
5. Frill on a sleeve
6. Outs' opponents
7. Scammed
8. Bull: Sp.
9. Brackish sea in Central Asia
10. Alexander Graham _____
11. "I don't give _____!"
12. Waiter's offering
13. Namesakes of Josip Broz
19. Sudan's continent: abbr.
20. Surrender abjectly
22. Greek island
25. Cheat
26. Fit
27. Loch _____ monster
28. Burrower
29. Alkaline's counterpart
30. Most August borns
31. Summer acquisition
32. Knotts or Meredith
33. Inlet
35. Fabrics
38. Dictionary entry: abbr.
42. Bret Harte's Chinese character
43. Hawaiian staple
44. Mister: Sp.

45. Kind of drum
46. Verdi's "_____ Miller"
47. Italian poet
48. Sicilian volcano
49. Kind of admiral

50. Small drinks
51. Aspen or pine
52. Let up
55. _____ Z

Answers on page 237.

MISH-MASH

ACROSS

1. Drag on board
9. It's often inset on US maps
15. Bowling, in the UK
16. Boston NBAer
17. Show interval
18. iPod, say
19. Red-pencils
20. Poetic night
22. Vocal vibrato
23. Fantastic birds
24. Frequent Wilder costar
26. Frozen dessert chain: abbr.
27. Distress signal
28. Asinine
30. Make lace
31. Kind of pear
32. Electronic music pioneer Edgard
34. Surfin' turf?
37. Polar sky phenomena
38. Stymied
39. Senator Specter
40. "_____ Rheingold"
41. Letters from college?
43. Hanoi holiday
46. Diminutive ending
48. _____ the head of the table
49. Like many people in Minn.
50. Word oft repeated by Pooh
52. Form of ID
53. Ballet rehearsal aid
54. _____ Pieces (candy)
56. Provided
58. "No question"
59. Down Under capital
60. Inventor's quest
61. "Why didn't I think of that!"

DOWN

1. Villainous looks
2. Indian native: var.
3. Silly behavior
4. Interjection of old
5. Transcript nos.
6. Word often seen among bubbles
7. Near the head
8. Baby talk?
9. Summer coolers: abbr.
10. Northern European
11. On the *qui vive*
12. Less lax
13. Polish meat product
14. Liturgical helpers
21. "Wayne's World" word
24. Writer of mysteries featuring Adam Dalgliesh
25. Stream
28. Not on good terms
29. Gives a hoot
31. Descriptive wd.
33. Director Howard
34. Welcome detour
35. Solemn denunciation
36. Superlatively mean
37. Phone number precursor?
39. Sourdough baker, for example
42. Violinist Shaham
43. Distended

44. Online broker
45. Poseidon's domain
47. Follow
49. Lieu for a luau

51. Adjust letter spacing in type
53. Run fast
55. Collector's quarry
57. Place to gambol

Answers on page 237.

FIRST LADIES

ACROSS

1. Birthplace of Lawrence Welk: abbr.
5. Ice cream purchase
9. Dallas school, for short
12. Prefix with space or stat
13. Quite some distance off
14. "_____ Wiedersehen"
15. First American woman in space
17. Rain-_____ (gum brand)
18. Hebrew title of respect for God
19. Monastery honcho
21. Mandela's land: abbr.
23. Suffer a humiliating loss, in slang
25. First female U.S. Secretary of Commerce
29. Joseph who started New York's Public Theater
30. Dull finish?
31. "PT 109" actor Robert
32. First child born in America to English parents
35. Fresh from the laundry
36. Antismoking gp.
37. Yaps
39. Put the finishing touches on
44. Christmas tree
45. First female Attorney General
47. Valuable deposit
48. Clashing forces?
49. Goddess pictured in Egyptian tombs
50. "Hmm . . . !?"
51. Causing a pucker
52. Pamper, with "on"

DOWN

1. Cape Canaveral gp.
2. Not working, as a battery
3. Guthrie who sang at Woodstock
4. Rhein port
5. Arrondissement resident
6. "_____ Ruled the World" (1965 hit)
7. Zapata's "zip"
8. Answer man?
9. Mole who takes action
10. _____ choice (test type)
11. Sky sight, supposedly
16. "The one that got away," say
20. It may come before lounger
22. Central courts
24. Cookbook amt.
25. Con
26. Went back on two legs, as a stallion
27. _____ Score (mnemonic method for testing newborns)
28. Actor born William Anderson
29. Popular pipe material, for short
33. Printer type
34. Zip
38. "Roots," e.g.
40. Very dry

24

41. Colombian coin
42. Knot or watt
43. Affectation

44. Egg _____ yung
46. Neither's companion

Answers on page 237.

TAKE YOUR VITAMINS

ACROSS

1. Animation collectible
4. Emerald, for one
7. The La _____ Tar Pits
11. OK, but not fabulous: hyph.
12. Lacto-_____-vegetarian
13. "Good _____" (Alton Brown show)
14. Made better
16. "Hedwig and the Angry _____"
17. With 14-ACROSS, function of vitamin D
19. Greek letter N's
20. Use binoculars
21. Sloe gin _____
24. Dix and Ticonderoga, e.g.: abbr.
25. Go head to head
28. With 14-ACROSS, function of vitamin K
32. Grosse _____, Michigan
33. Payback without the payback
34. Put up a picture
35. "_____ the ramparts we watched..."
36. Salt Lake City collegiate athlete
38. With 14-ACROSS, function of vitamin C
44. Inkling
45. With 14-ACROSS, function of vitamin A
46. Bug attracted to flames
47. Jeremy Piven's "Entourage" role
48. _____ ex machina
49. _____ bargaining
50. Movie studio film site
51. Antiquated word meaning "old"

DOWN

1. Crooner Perry
2. "SportsCenter" network
3. Actor Lamas
4. They have authority over the state or country: abbr.
5. In perpetuity
6. California home of the E. & J. Gallo Winery
7. Brownish neutral shade
8. Go off on a loud tangent
9. _____ A Sketch
10. Volcano spew
11. Bro or sis, for short
15. School where Craig Robinson, brother of Michelle Obama, is the men's basketball coach: abbr.
18. Egg holder?
21. Group with a warning on VHS tapes and DVDs: abbr.
22. Under the weather
23. Yellowy-orange "Sesame Street" muppet
24. H1N1, for instance
25. By means of
26. Overnight stopover
27. Quiche ingredient

29. "*Mon* _____!" (French outburst)
30. Eye parts
31. Where dressing is served for some salads, with "on"
35. Home of Nebraska's largest zoo
36. "_____ wisely"
37. Baseball legend Cobb and footballer Law, for two
38. "American _____" (show with judge Randy Jackson)
39. Portion (out)
40. Charlotte Brontë heroine Jane
41. Neutrogena medicated shampoo: hyph.
42. Former Israeli prime minister Olmert
43. Adirondack components: abbr.
44. Little rapscallion

 Answers on page 237.

BACKSTORY

ACROSS

1. Sign in Duffy Square (just north of Times Square)
5. Bygone flyer: abbr.
8. Take away, in a way
12. "I'll try _____ bit"
13. Actress/model Carrere
14. Rebecca of the WNBA
15. Loser in a famous race
16. "Sure, why not?"
18. Designer paid his way through college by working in restaurants
20. "A mouse!"
21. "Cool to the core" brand
26. Past
29. Old Ford model
31. "No Passing" is one
32. Designer who once wrote for "Vogue Italia"
36. He played Jack on "30 Rock"
37. What the doctor might want you to say
38. Volcano output
39. Court figure
42. Just put a bit (on)
44. Designer who was captain of her high school tennis team
49. Central element of a hit Fox TV show
53. Item designed by 16-, 32-, or 44-ACROSS
54. Where men are from, supposedly
55. Big-12 home of the Cowgirls: abbr.
56. Kansas, from 1854 to 1861: abbr.
57. Leap and a spin
58. Line part: abbr.
59. Small batteries

DOWN

1. Actor and singer Mowry
2. Fictional river in 1957 movie
3. George W. Bush had one more than his father
4. Famous line in The Who's "Tommy"
5. Adhere: 2 wds.
6. Sound of relief
7. Unstable subatomic particle
8. "Kidnapped" monogram
9. The dawn goddess in Greek literature
10. Airer of Julia Child's "The French Chef" from 1963-1973
11. "Hollywood Squares" win
17. Abbr. in a help wanted ad
19. Make yourself hoarse, perhaps
22. "Quiet!": var.
23. She played Liz on "30 Rock"
24. Auspices
25. Egyptian symbol used in modern jewelry
26. Key of Mozart's "Piano Sonata No. 11": abbr.
27. Family name in "The Wizard of Oz"

28. Georges
30. Abbr. used by many sole proprietors
33. Birth month of most Libras: abbr.
34. Technically, it's a beetle, and there's a 50-50 chance it's male
35. Melville's captain
40. Yadda, roughly: abbr.
41. Stacked caramel snacks
43. Rhymes of rap
45. Dodge

46. Caroline who was the first host of "The Biggest Loser"
47. Mrs. Dithers in "Blondie" comics
48. Letters on a towel
49. Show hosted by Robin Roberts and George Stephanopoulos: abbr.
50. Not strict
51. Center of a famous palindrome
52. One way to learn the language: abbr.

Answers on page 238.

ON THE TREE

ACROSS

1. Online journals
6. Top gun
9. Show of deference
12. Yankee Yogi
13. Neighbor of Swed.
14. Segment of history
15. Talk-show host O'Brien
16. Sparklers for the tree
18. Lemon follower
19. Design with acid
20. Highland hats
22. Overhead RRs
23. Nile snakes
27. Hot temper
28. _____ Moines, IA
29. Bit of tomfoolery
30. Foil for the tree
32. Rival of the tree
33. River of Hades
34. Angora or Burmese
35. Lamb's father
36. "Lohengrin" lass
37. New Jersey cape
38. What's more
39. Tender cut
41. Wallach of "Lord Jim"
42. Loops for the tree
45. Snug
48. Lennon's widow
49. Part of AT&T
50. Sneeze sound
51. Coloring agent
52. Clod chopper
53. Stop gripping

DOWN

1. U.K. channel
2. Zodiac's only carnivore
3. Spheres for the tree
4. Alums
5. *Compos mentis*
6. Harpists for the tree
7. Young horses
8. _____ the Red
9. Wager
10. Lode load
11. Card game for two
17. Scottish feudal lord
20. Book ID
21. Disney mermaid
22. Lamprey
24. Topper for the tree
25. Gyro breads
26. Likable loser
28. Ruby of "A Raisin in the Sun"
29. Creative skill
31. "We _____ Overcome"
32. Manner
34. Light for the tree, once
37. Sal of "Rebel Without a Cause"
38. Wonderland visitor
40. Swear word
41. & others: Lat.
42. Zeus or Jupiter
43. Indefinite amount
44. Fish eggs
46. Glutton
47. Besides

Answers on page 238.

BANG FOR THE BUCK

ACROSS

1. Not-so-big shot?
4. Fraternity party staple
7. Hex
12. Comical Costello
13. Commotion
14. Circa
15. "_____ the ramparts . . ."
16. Dovetail
17. Sounds of agony
18. Win a lot of money
21. Uninteresting
22. He pitied the fool
23. Spread on bread
25. Keydets' school: abbr.
26. _____-fi
29. Get lucky while gambling
33. GI cops: abbr.
34. Cries of disappointment
35. Con votes
36. West Bank group: abbr.
37. Former Euopean airline: abbr.
39. Clean up
44. Unconcerned
45. Weapon for Wile E. Coyote: abbr.
46. Hugs in a love letter
47. Shearer of the silver screen
48. Sensitive subject, to some
49. Hyperlinked item, often: abbr.
50. Hope for addicts, for short
51. Rocky outcrop
52. Set eyes on

DOWN

1. Lump
2. War that Arthur Conan Doyle served in
3. Certainties
4. "The Metamorphosis" author
5. Author Wharton
6. Barbarian
7. Cotton cloth
8. WWII menace: hyph.
9. Bay sprinkled with white, e.g.
10. Like a ship on the ocean floor
11. Space aliens, for short
19. Tons
20. Austen novel
23. Eponymous physicist
24. Collagen injection site
25. MTV hosts, for short
26. Roomy
27. Reluctant
28. Roy Orbison's "_____ Over"
30. Nova Scotia's capital
31. "Return of the Jedi" creature
32. Bark-covered bulge
36. Merchandising scheme, briefly
37. Game-winning shout
38. Streamlined swimmer
39. Fruity gin flavoring
40. Libel or fraud
41. Louisiana, to Louis
42. Apple discard
43. Flaw in logic
44. &

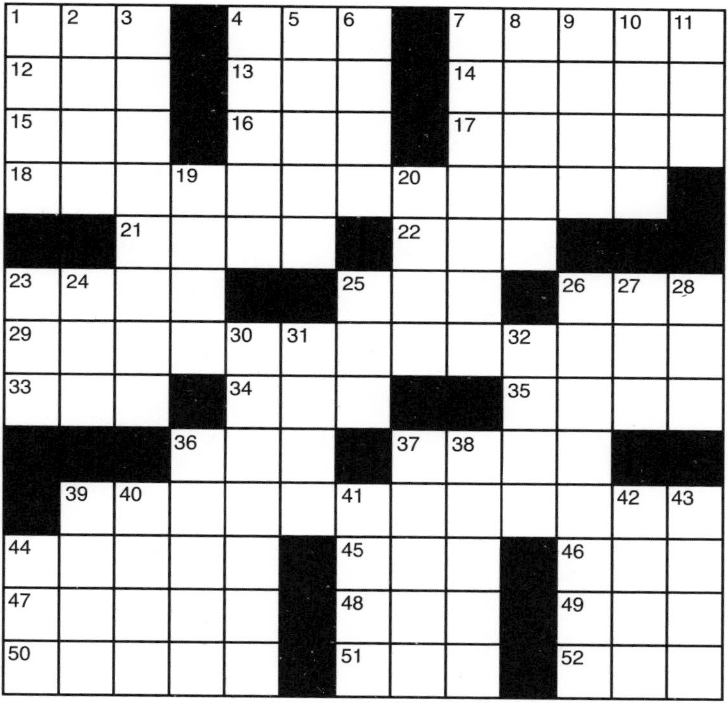

Answers on page 238.

I DON'T LIKE MONDAYS

ACROSS

1. Town
5. "Norma _____" (Sally Field film)
8. Rapidly
12. Hydrox look-alike
13. Right-angled pipe
14. Golden Spike locale
15. Kind of
17. Investment firm T. _____ Price
18. Rules govering caviar?
20. "Snug as _____ . . ."
21. Aim (to)
22. ". . . to buy _____ pig"
23. High-end speaker brand
25. Superlative ending
28. Evil flying insect?
31. "Fine!" astronaut-style: hyph.
32. Prefix for plasm
33. Sci-fi vehicles, for short
34. Durable wood
35. Deliberate slight
36. Priority customers?
41. Think-tank product
42. Bar with a polar bear logo
45. Eden dweller
46. Philosopher's study
47. Vacationer in a camper, informally
48. Mystery writer Paretsky
49. Highlander's negative
50. Safecracker, in slang

DOWN

1. "Sk8er _____" (2002 Avril Lavigne hit)
2. Java holder
3. Wind up for a big punch
4. Migrate, say
5. Tear
6. Likewise
7. Makes a choice about
8. Like an Ewok
9. Tours "yours"
10. Like cut wood
11. Friend's addressee
16. Head lines?: abbr.
19. _____ frog
20. High hairstyle
22. Battery size
23. Tanned jacket material
24. Polo Grounds superstar Mel
25. Overflowing
26. Messy eater
27. Cobb and Pennington
29. Male escort
30. Becomes nonproductive
34. Bush successor
35. One of 100 in D.C.: abbr.
36. Rondo and Rio
37. Norse poem
38. 2010, e.g.
39. Rick's love in "Casablanca"
40. City on Norton Sound
43. Bud holder?
44. Dyne-centimeter

Answers on page 238.

ACROSS

1. "Invasion of the Body Snatchers" container
4. Agency worker, for short
8. Speak up?
12. Preserves container
13. Comic strip pooch
14. Corn Belt state
15. Jamaica-based music
16. Animal in a Gelett Burgess poem
18. Nintendo debut of 2006
20. Ever: 2 wds.
21. Drink containing pineapple juice
26. "_____ to differ"
27. Nosegay
28. Chronic complainer
31. "Bye-bye"
32. Basketball's path
33. "_____ Lisa"
34. Kazakhstan, once: abbr.
35. Bond villain
36. Diner sign
37. Crispy snack item
39. Campfire remnant
42. Like some tapes: abbr.
43. "Juke Box Baby" singer
47. Drivers' organization: abbr.
50. Divas have big ones
51. Mata of spydom
52. Gramophone speed: abbr.
53. Serenity
54. Like ideal cactus climate
55. Very important

DOWN

1. Some flannels, briefly
2. Former acorn
3. Approach
4. Conversation fodder
5. End of a student's e-mail address, often
6. Soviet space outpost
7. Gusto
8. Madonna-and-child depiction
9. Cape _____ (westernmost point of continental Europe)
10. No-show GI: abbr.
11. Two-masted craft
17. Tramp's love
19. 1995 role for Branagh
21. Snapshots, for short
22. Sacred bird
23. Eyeball-bending genre
24. Ms. Doone
25. Type of tie
28. Biblical floating zoo
29. Dead set against
30. Sudden inhalation
33. Kind of engineer: abbr.
35. Blue fish in "Finding Nemo"
37. Taken alone
38. Not perfectly round
39. Olympics sword
40. Prefix with phone or byte
41. Family business abbreviation, often
44. Dance start
45. Dinghy blade
46. Noninvasive medical procedure: abbr.
48. One rung on the evolutionary ladder
49. "Doubt" actress Adams

Answers on page 238.

ICE SQUAD

ACROSS

1. Actor Waterston
4. Protective ditch
8. Highest point
12. Pizza order
13. Earthenware crock
14. Neighbor of Vietnam
15. Hawaiian or Tahitian, e.g.
17. Mayberry kid
18. Obscures
19. Greek letter
20. Meddler
21. Forum VIP
25. Albert Pinkham and Winona
27. Hustle and bustle
28. Catch a glimpse of
31. Nocturnal bird
32. Killed violently
33. Get the point
34. Disney dwarf
36. Black leopard
38. Some Semites
42. Regular Joe
43. Trademark scrubber
44. Name of 12 popes
46. Victimizer
48. Actor Estrada
49. Graph or mat lead-in
50. Scull propeller
51. Kitchen utensils
52. Penn or Connery
53. Pig pen

DOWN

1. Hot, in a way
2. Theater passageway
3. Cantaloupe, e.g.
4. Weekend follower
5. Early carmaker
6. Tavern brew
7. Roofer's gunk
8. Waikiki greeting
9. Government seat
10. Pierre, to Pierre
11. Suffix for a language
16. Singing cowboy Gene
19. Brain, spinal cord, etc.: abbr.
21. Waste conduit
22. _____ Stanley Gardner
23. Poem of praise
24. Horizontal lineup
26. Loser to Clinton in 1996
28. Psychic letters
29. Kind of horse or cow
30. Antarctic bird
32. Damascus land
34. Like a wallflower
35. Absolution
37. Walrus teeth
39. Chorus members
40. Become swollen
41. Rueful
43. Letter after alpha
44. Energy
45. Levin or Gershwin
46. Family men
47. Be penitent

Answers on page 238.

ACROSS

1. Bodychecked, say
4. Drink with body
8. _____ Boxer, first American-born player drafted to the NHL
12. His number 4 jersey was retired by the Bruins
13. Party to a pact
14. Hodgepodge
15. Fight ender: abbr.
16. 1981–82 Conn Smythe Trophy winner
18. Notebook projection
20. Vichyssoise ingredients
21. Three-time Conn Smythe Trophy winner
26. St. Louis Blues captain Brewer (2008–11)
27. Not of the clergy
28. Mu _____ pork
31. Czech hockey player Hemsky, or some 4-ACROSSES
32. Court organization: abbr.
33. Papal name
34. Rocky crag
35. Very dry, as champagne
36. Resourceful
37. 1976–77 Conn Smythe Trophy winner
39. Animal trail
42. "The Star-Spangled Banner" preposition
43. 1970–71 Conn Smythe Trophy winner
47. Pen filler
50. Analogy chunk
51. The NCAA's Hockey _____
52. Blackjack high card
53. Not worth debating
54. Band aids?
55. Yule drink

DOWN

1. Just off the grill
2. Get one's dander up
3. NHL Rookie of the Year in 1975–76
4. Thumper's chum
5. Peyton's quarterback brother
6. Grazer whose name is Shawnee for "white"
7. Grain in some whiskey
8. Poppycock
9. Word suggesting options
10. Take chances
11. Young men
17. Voting group
19. Ball trajectories
21. Dry fuel
22. Folk's Guthrie
23. Robert of "Hogan's Heroes"
24. Khyber Pass city
25. Gaucho's lariat
28. _____ husky (certain sled dog)
29. Internet source for TV programs
30. Internet searcher, e.g.
33. Wan

35. Third vice president Aaron _____

37. Vladimir and Estragon waited for him
38. Adobe offerings
39. Two percent alternative
40. 100 *centavos*

41. Not oblivious of
44. Passing need?
45. Racing form datum
46. Mind-reading, briefly
48. Cpl. or sgt.
49. Gunpowder container

Answers on page 239.

ONLINE ENNUI

ACROSS

1. Chinese tea
4. 1960 world chess champ Mikhail
7. Scoundrel
10. Be unwell
11. "Last Essays of _____": Lamb
13. Carlos's house
14. TV shows
16. Discoverer of heavy hydrogen, Harold _____
17. Words of wisdom: Part I
19. Where Bourg is
20. Shrinking sea
21. Uprising
24. Folk singer DiFranco
25. Savings plan: abbr.
28. Words of wisdom: Part II
32. "Wow!"
33. Road along Lake Michigan in Chicago: abbr.
34. Homeowner's hangover?
35. Legal plea, briefly
37. D.C. time
39. Words of wisdom: Part III
45. Darkness, in Dijon
46. Detect
47. Metric weight
48. "Able was I _____ saw Elba"
49. Anti-smoking org.
50. Lawrence and Louis: abbr.
51. Year abroad: Sp.
52. Wealthy Londoner

DOWN

1. Matador's cloak
2. Big name in Dixieland jazz
3. Spiky-leaved plant
4. Country singer Gibbs
5. Actor Delon
6. Arm or leg
7. Home of the Panthers
8. Candidate for rehab
9. Bigmouth Martha
12. Diagonal
13. Where the USS Maine was sunk
15. Bar chart
18. Iroquois foe
21. Ratchet
22. Pee Wee Reese's retired number
23. Fork and spoon
24. Linking word
26. Speed (up)
27. Chowed down
29. She outwrestled Thor
30. Tristan's beloved
31. Fashionably nostalgic
36. Sarge Snorkel's dog
37. He was Jed Clampett
38. Prefix for path or political
39. Blotter blots
40. Outfit
41. Pre-euro coin
42. Novelist Turgenev
43. Pixar clownfish
44. Smash and _____

Answers on page 239.

STEP LIVELY

ACROSS

1. Window sticker
6. Whole ball of wax
9. Chance introduction?
12. Girl of "Paint Your Wagon" song
13. Tiny legume
14. Canton bordering Lake of Lucerne
15. Matzo or pita
17. "Good Will Hunting" school: abbr.
18. Atlas line
19. "Maid in Manhattan" star
21. Chaperon
24. The latest
25. Bee Gee's disco voice
27. Nits to pick
30. WBA stat
31. Like an April day
33. Devilfish
34. Birthdate determines it
36. Missile part
38. Lacunae
40. "Thank U" singer Morissette
41. Alpha's opposite
43. Reformers' targets
44. The old block?
45. Where to find the first parts of 15-A, 9-D, and 23-DOWN
50. Down Under bird
51. King in the 1922 news
52. Shakespearean spirit
53. Fall guy
54. Org. for arguers?
55. Parkway payments

DOWN

1. Cool, to rappers
2. House addition
3. Org. in Clancy novels
4. Houston ball club
5. Hand
6. Made a good impression?
7. Grassland
8. Soup server
9. Lifts weights
10. Weird lake?
11. Hotel name
16. Patio furniture materials
20. Hogwarts messenger
21. Red salamanders
22. "Tobermory" author
23. Obstructed, like a drain
24. Like merchandise at full price
26. Mom's brother in Mazatlan
28. "Pretty please?"
29. Gazes
32. Tells off, and then some
35. Belmont loser
37. Cuban dictator
39. Pappardelle, e.g.
41. Horace wrote 88
42. Doll's cry
43. Minute amount
46. Center of activity
47. Peak _____
48. Aunt or uncle: abbr.
49. Dolly has two

Answers on page 239.

COMPUTER CINEMA

ACROSS

1. Londoner's slicker
4. Train unit
7. Touched down
11. "How was _____ know?"
12. Claude Akins role, Sheriff _____
13. NASA's first lady in orbit
14. Postal motto word
15. He played Obi Wan
16. Straw in the wind
17. Movie of 1995 based on a computer game
20. Yokohama drama
21. Koufax had a low one: abbr.
22. Melville mariner
24. Fill to the gills
26. Soccer star Hamm
29. Computer-runs-amok movie of 1970, "Colossus: The _____"
32. Give it a go
33. Lauder competitor
34. Falco of "Nurse Jackie"
35. Chapel seat
36. Half a cocktail
37. Computer nerd movie of 1985
43. *Urbi et* _____ ("to the City and to the World," in old Rome")
44. Concrete
45. Suffix with chlor-
47. Nothing, in Nantes
48. Resistance units
49. Edge out
50. Waiting-room call
51. Bambi's aunt
52. Letter from Greece

DOWN

1. Part of an hour: abbr.
2. It's split at CERN
3. From the heart
4. Pop without kids
5. Director Ferrara
6. Goddard "fathered" this science
7. Bouquet
8. Precarious perch
9. Sometimes a great notion
10. Jamboree sight
12. Plaster backing
18. LBJ in-law
19. Commercial cookie
22. Rudder locale
23. Opposite of vertical: abbr.
24. Winter footwear
25. Appropriate
26. Part of D.V.M.
27. Here, in Paris
28. Had a snack
30. Treated a sprain, maybe
31. Capt. _____-Luc Picard
35. Kind of journalism
36. Danson and Koppel
37. Like a favorite shirt
38. Buffalo's lake
39. Eurasian goat
40. "Call Me Irresponsible" lyricist Sammy

41. Thomas of blues
42. Delete a scene
46. They banned DDT: abbr.

1	2	3		4	5	6		7	8	9	10
11				12				13			
14				15				16			
	17		18				19				
	20					21					
22	23				24	25				26	27	28
29				30				31			
32				33				34			
		35				36				
37	38	39			40	41			42	
43				44				45		46
47				48				49		
50				51				52		

Answers on page 239.

AT ONE'S BIDDING

ACROSS

1. *In medias* _____
4. In pieces
9. PIN requester: abbr.
12. Yellowstone herd member
13. Object of art
14. Nintendo game console
15. 1940 war film starring Robert Taylor
18. Track competitions
19. Killer whale
20. Targeted, with "at"
22. Shoreline recesses
24. Writer born in Boston in 1809
25. Saudi Arabia city
27. Office request
33. Monopoly player's payments
34. Two-way preposition
35. Andromeda, for one
38. Songwriters' group: abbr.
40. Pindar poems
41. Promenade, in Pamplona
43. Gratis
48. Classic start?
49. Pointless
50. "What can brown do for you?" company: abbr.
51. Connecticut's WNBA team
52. Comes up short
53. Hiker's guide

DOWN

1. Foul caller
2. Pipe type
3. Pool tool
4. Needed Tylenol, perhaps
5. Golf shot
6. Story lines
7. _____ de Janeiro
8. He's a turkey
9. Omniscient
10. Touch of color
11. Greedy king of myth
16. "Gosh!"
17. Wisdom tooth
20. Software solution, briefly
21. Debt reminder
22. Finishes cakes: abbr.
25. Oodles of
26. Round figure: abbr.
28. Stock market downturn
29. Do voodoo
30. Politeness
31. Pitching stat: abbr.
32. House member: abbr.
35. Prom apparel
36. Parting remark
37. Revealed one's true feelings
38. Signs of a fire
39. Hemingway novel setting
41. School groups: abbr.
42. Benzoyl peroxide target
44. "Black gold"
45. Game with Reverse cards
46. School stat: abbr.
47. Clairvoyance, for example: abbr.

Answers on page 239.

MUSIC FIT FOR A KING

ACROSS

1. When repeated, a Yale cheer
6. Come to the plate
9. Lively folk dance
12. Case for a gastroenterologist
13. "Well, looky here!"
14. Flap, so to speak
15. Clinic's work, at times
16. Genre of many an MC
17. Food fish
18. 1958 Nat King Cole song
21. Early Beatles member Sutcliffe
22. Fencer in a mask
25. Country club organization: abbr.
28. Norse verse collection
31. Having two parts
32. 1961 Nat King Cole song
35. Gymnastic cushions
36. Notable time spans
37. "You rang?"
38. Smooth, in a way
40. Paris byway
42. 1962 Nat King Cole song
48. Repartee
50. Kick _____ fuss
51. Combat gear
52. Pseudonymous letters
53. Fabled bird
54. Smart group
55. Nero Wolfe creator Stout
56. Service charge
57. Blithering sort

DOWN

1. Actor-singer Ives
2. Spreadable stick
3. *Cuatro y cuatro*
4. Plumbing problems
5. Umpire
6. 1976–80 Wimbledon champ
7. Ishmael's commander
8. Fall birthstone
9. Notorious figure of November 1963
10. Bachelor's last words?
11. "If _____ did not exist . . .": Voltaire
19. Give an elbow
20. End notes?
23. Smoker's lung sound
24. Corrida encouragements
25. Ship's engine part
26. Growl
27. Net, in a way
29. German "the," for masculine nouns
30. Nintendo predecessor
33. Greek mount
34. Result of undersea activity
39. Blue cartoon character
41. Missed the mark
43. Fraternal organization: abbr.
44. Dainty trim
45. Dodge model introduced in 1978
46. Leaving something to be desired: hyph.

47. Part of QED
48. Two-person card game
49. Kyle's baby brother, on "South Park"

1	2	3	4	5	■	6	7	8	■	9	10	11
12					■	13			■	14		
15					■	16			■	17		
18				19				20		■	■	■
■	■	21			■	■	22			23	24
25	26	27	■	28		29	30	■	31			
32			33				34					
35				■	36				■	37		
38				39	■	■	40		41	■	■	■
■	■	42			43	44				45	46	47
48	49		■	50			■	51				
52			■	53			■	54				
55			■	56			■	57				

Answers on page 239.

MONSTER HEADS

ACROSS

1. Shaft
4. One way to run
9. "See you later!"
12. Office casual day: abbr.
13. Lake near Squaw Valley
14. Bagel's partner
15. Flitting insect
17. "To Spring," e.g.
18. Country singer Tillis
19. Medical emetic
21. Tram
25. She-lobster
26. _____ Miguel (largest of the Azores)
27. Eminem contemporary
31. Does the math
33. Barge pusher
35. Tournament draw
36. Violinist's application
38. Prefix with realism
40. Put paper into, as a copier
41. Italian blue cheese
44. H's position in the alphabet
47. Ask for a handout
48. Marseilles Mrs.: abbr.
49. Shrub with showy flowers
54. Stain
55. Signs to heed
56. It contains albumen and vitellus
57. The Tin Man's prop
58. It may be present
59. "Winnie-the-Pooh" baby

DOWN

1. Postal letters: abbr.
2. Former NHL great Bobby
3. "Lucy in the Sky With _____"
4. Many of the Marshall Islands
5. Isle of _____
6. Channels above 13, once: abbr.
7. Infant's woe
8. ATM part
9. Group, as of votes
10. Old Jedi
11. Small businessman?
16. Hair-care product
20. Goes astray
21. "_____ she blows!"
22. Change the furnishings
23. Devour
24. Not old
28. Windshield clearer
29. Film holder
30. Collection of Old Norse poems
32. Melancholic sound
34. Tracker or Prizm maker
37. No longer in
39. At first, perhaps
42. Hop, for Pop
43. Kind of Buddhism
44. Actress Thompson or Samms
45. Film format with a huge screen
46. "Chicago" star of 2002

50. Place for a recliner
51. ICU figures: abbr.
52. Diva quality
53. "All Those Years _____"
    (George Harrison hit)

1	2	3		4	5	6	7	8		9	10	11
12				13						14		
15			16							17		
		18					19		20			
21	22				23	24						
25				26				27		28	29	30
31			32		33		34		35			
36				37		38		39		40		
			41		42				43			
44	45	46						47				
48				49		50	51				52	53
54				55						56		
57				58						59		

Answers on page 240.

LOG-IN INFORMATION

ACROSS

1. "Dear" ones
5. Old PC platform: abbr.
8. DNA collector, perhaps
12. Savings partner
13. Geologic time period
14. Life saver
15. 11,000-foot Italian peak
16. Symbol of industriousness
17. Come (from)
18. Ragamuffin
19. Hawaiian wreath
20. Gained a lap
21. First piece of data needed to log in to a chat room, say
25. Camp sight
28. Give it a whirl
29. Corporate department
32. Break
34. Run of luck
35. Antiquated
36. "_____ Loves You"
37. Like some martinis
38. Second piece of data needed to log in to a chat room, say
41. Dude
43. "And I Love _____"
44. Frolic
48. Character
50. Food scrap
51. Domain
52. Olympian's blade
53. "The Three Faces of _____"
54. Cause of some quaking
55. Computer support?
56. Lion's home
57. Honky-_____

DOWN

1. Boatload
2. Itty-bitty bit
3. Hindu princess
4. Big mess
5. Some casino staff
6. Cantankerous
7. Gown material
8. "Put a lid on it!"
9. Scammed one's way out of
10. Soprano's song, maybe
11. Hightail it
22. Overwhelms
23. Fall flower
24. Fold, spindle or mutilate
25. Comedienne Margaret
26. Painter's medium
27. Future frogs
30. Canal locale
31. Sun spot?
33. It may be high in the afternoon
34. Abbreviate
36. Turn suddenly
39. Did a blacksmith's job
40. Word before beer or dodger
41. Partner of born
42. Climbing gear
45. Creme-filled cookie
46. Ill-tempered
47. Part of PRNDL
49. It's a scream

54

Answers on page 240.

THERE AUTO BE A LAW

ACROSS

1. Ford and Lincoln, but not Obama
5. One who says yes to an offer
13. "A Prayer for _____ Meany"
14. Rich: 3 wds.
15. Pre-stereo
16. Overdid the flattery
17. Show affection from afar
19. Not straight
20. Snopes.com topic
24. Cheap cigar
28. Brief vacation
30. Hound
32. Like old grease
33. Plaintiff
35. Norman Vincent _____
36. Hockey score
37. Back of the neck
39. Some shooting stars?
44. Dope
48. Pigeon-_____
49. Two-player hoops game
50. Able to see right through
51. One who fiddles (with)
52. Happy _____

DOWN

1. Rooster topper
2. Missing from the Marines, say
3. Comedy Central's "_____ 911!"
4. Falling flakes
5. Open-eyed
6. Giving up, as territory
7. Small bunch
8. Some wings
9. Class-conscious grp.
10. "Sesame Street" watcher
11. "_____ to Billie Joe"
12. Casting requirement?
18. Vast chasm
20. Luxuriant tresses
21. Female empowerment group: abbr.
22. Horse's longest hair
23. Jekyll's alter ego
24. Choppy hairdo
25. _____ Bell
26. Black-and-white predator
27. France, before it was France
29. Narrow down
31. One awash in bills?
34. Plunder
38. Indiana basketballer
39. Corn _____
40. _____ Ant, 1960s cartoon superhero
41. Certain basketball defense
42. Epsilon follower
43. TV's "American _____"
44. "_____ so fast!"
45. Gasteyer of "Mean Girls"
46. "Losing My Religion" rock group
47. One with a beat

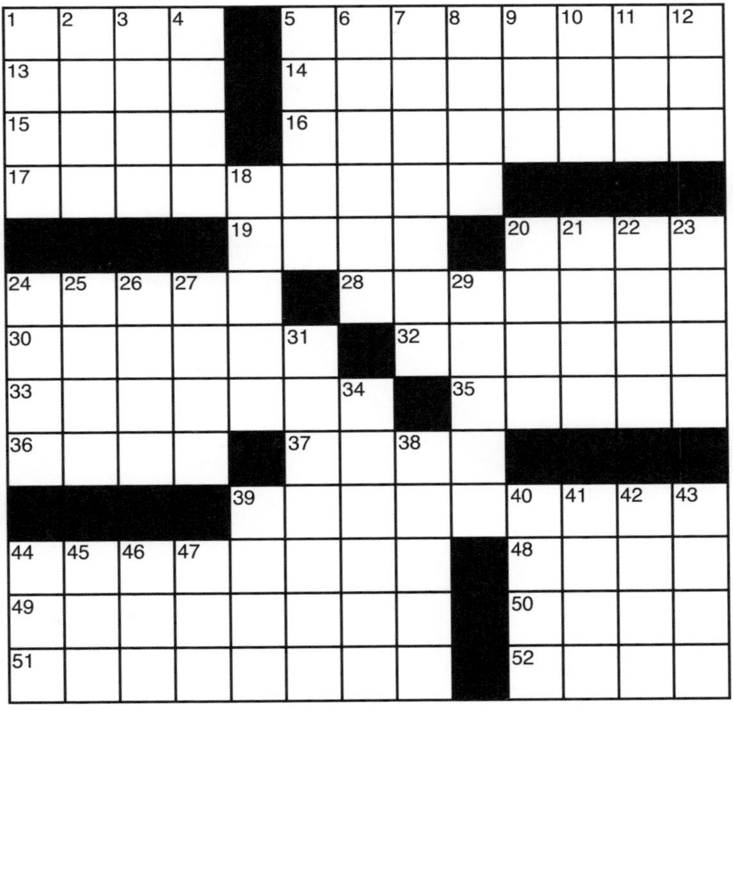

Answers on page 240.

SOCIAL NETWORKING

ACROSS

1. Omelet essentials
5. What you can do if you don't know the words
8. Excellent, in modern slang
12. Pirate's booty
13. "_____ questions?"
14. Extremely popular
15. Compos mentis
16. U.N. workers' group: abbr.
17. Doomsayer's sign
18. Guitarist for U2, with "The"
19. Swindle, slangily, with "off"
20. Low voice
21. Professional social networking site launched in 2003
24. Punk rock offshoot
27. Meet with
28. Indian yogurt dip
31. Chewy candy
33. Flock leader
34. Aquarium fish
35. Rainbow shape
36. "Is it soup _____?"
37. Friendship-oriented social networking site launched in 2004
40. Public relations effort
42. Cambridge university: abbr.
43. Handouts
47. Follow
48. Flowery verse
49. Carrot, e.g.
50. Capri, e.g.
51. Gumshoe
52. Stag
53. Connecting point
54. "C'_____ la vie!"
55. From square one

DOWN

1. "...or _____!"
2. Egg on
3. "The _____ Show" (1970s TV show hosted by Chuck Barris)
4. Girder material
5. Cafeteria headwear
6. Dissimilar
7. Mr. Magoo, e.g.
8. Irrational fears
9. "Oh, the _____!": phrase used to describe the Hindenburg disaster
10. Census data
11. Column next to the ones
22. Newton or Stern
23. _____ Malfoy, Harry Potter's nemesis
24. Medical specialty: abbr.
25. Stooge with a bowl cut
26. Long way from home?
29. Piggy
30. Public hanging?
32. Spanish nobleman
33. "To serve and _____," motto written on the side of police cruisers
35. Puts up with
38. Be theatrical
39. Payback, in Buddhism

40. Knee/ankle connector
41. Cancún coin
44. Student aid, say

45. C.I.A. worry
46. Slow-cooker fare

1	2	3	4		5	6	7		8	9	10	11
12					13				14			
15					16				17			
18					19				20			
			21	22				23				
24	25	26		27				28			29	30
31			32				33					
34					35				36			
		37			38				39			
40	41				42				43	44	45	46
47					48				49			
50					51				52			
53					54				55			

Answers on page 240.

MOUTHPIECES

ACROSS

1. Inc., in England
4. Kind of herring
8. Paint layer
12. Road-debris protection
13. "Big _____" (David Ortiz nickname)
14. Lord over
15. Boy Scout bash
17. Superimposed on
18. Shrewish quality
20. Halloween trick, e.g.
23. Crystal-lined rock
24. Rodeo ropee
25. Word before number or forwarding
28. Sign of resolve
34. Spheres
35. Tom Harkin's state
36. Dog on "The Jetsons"
40. Luminous
41. Craving for dessert
45. Chicken piece
46. Soup choice
50. Hostile to
51. Flake (off)
52. On your face, it's embarrassing
53. Untouchable leader?
54. Nae sayer
55. Madhouse

DOWN

1. JFK's successor
2. Part of a chorus line?
3. See 36-DOWN
4. Kirk's enterprise mate
5. Mata _____
6. Imitated
7. Limit one's caloric intake
8. Heavy lifter
9. Expenditure
10. For the whole world to hear
11. Conical dwelling
16. Canadian National Park
19. Eyeball an eyeful
20. Some workstations: abbr.
21. Mob pariah
22. Louisville slugger?
25. Dog catcher's quarry
26. Police radio alert, briefly
27. Music collector's stack
29. Kind of print or soldier
30. Accurate
31. Modern joke response: abbr.
32. _____ Jima
33. Cat foot
36. Nile obstacle, with 3-DOWN
37. Cast pearls before _____
38. Campers' homes
39. Talk show fixture Philbin
40. Like the Leaning Tower of Pisa
42. Cookbook abbr.
43. Cartel of 12 countries: abbr.
44. Faux dairy stick
47. Candy from a head?
48. Swelled head
49. Long, long _____

Answers on page 240.

IN POSITION

ACROSS

1. Plagued with turbulence
6. Glove compartment item
9. Simple bunk
12. Precursor to Nintendo
13. Exploit
14. Acorn producer
15. Attacking
18. "Star Trek" villain
19. Automatic reponse
20. "_____ la la..."
22. Uses scissors
25. OR hook-ups
28. Predisposed opinion
31. "Seven Gothic Tales" author Dinesen
32. Well-off
35. "What gives?"
36. War of the Roses house
37. Word before "loves me" and "loves me not"
38. Tortilla chip topper
40. Bettor's slip
42. Try to fix
45. Rocket launcher
49. Boxer's respite
52. Start of many a Catholic church name
53. Poem of praise
54. Brown-coated ermine
55. Cpl.'s superior
56. Map lines: abbr.
57. Jazzy Lee

DOWN

1. Refuse to act
2. 45th U.S. state
3. Author Angelou
4. Word processor command
5. Female force
6. Guiding genius
7. "You wish!"
8. Suffers from sunburn
9. Has peaceful relations (with)
10. Granola piece
11. Ref's declaration
16. Like some enlarged photos
17. Aladdin's discovery
21. Hitter's stat.
23. Lane
24. Terrier type
25. Goddess pictured in Egyptian tombs
26. Traveler's O.K.
27. Valiant
29. "It's _____!" (thumbs-up reply)
30. Vernal equinox follower
33. He lost his title to Douglas in 1990
34. Big initials in old films
39. Fire of the mind
41. Join
43. Mavericks star Jason
44. Components of elevens
46. Full of anticipation
47. Type of carpet
48. Legal rep.

49. May day!
50. Harbor craft
51. Sci-fi talent

Answers on page 240.

BEAT IT!

ACROSS

1. "Vamoose!"
6. Land
13. Football's _____ Bowl
14. Elvis _____, the King of Rock
15. Bedouin, e.g.
16. Touchy?
17. Sixth sense, for short
18. Tiny organism: var.
20. Hi-_____ monitor
21. Muppet who once claimed, "Moi hair has natural curls. So does my tail."
26. Go to a different state?
27. Scourge
28. Top-of-the-line
31. College grounds
33. Gelatin substitute
34. 1986 graphic novel depicting Art Spiegelman's father's escape from the Nazis
35. Golden ticket holders?
38. CEO's degree
41. Flowing tresses
42. Bobby of hockey
43. Cameo
47. Green Day album and Broadway play, "American _____"
49. Pilot
50. New money on the Continent
51. Loggins's 1970s musical partner
52. Poorly kept

DOWN

1. Not as crazy
2. Within walking distance, say
3. Frolics
4. "I get it!"
5. "Portrait of _____," infamous painting by John Singer Sargent
6. Best suited
7. Old joke: "Do you serve _____ here?" "Yes sir, we serve everybody!"
8. Rundown
9. N.Y.C. clock setting
10. Rhyming boxing champ
11. Hair goo
12. CBS logo
19. "8 _____," 2002 semi-autobiographical film starring Eminem
22. Some PCs
23. Cumberland _____
24. Wildebeest
25. Sycophant's answer
26. Darkness
28. Black bird
29. Bigheadedness
30. PC linkup
31. Give a darn
32. Pals from Perth, say
34. "Om," e.g.
36. Fine fiddle
37. Red _____ (Snoopy's nemesis)
38. Wavelike design

39. Ones a mother hen mothers
40. Like craft shows
43. "Kapow!"
44. "_____ fallen . . ."

45. Frank McCourt memoir of 1999
46. _____ de deux
48. Expected

Answers on page 241.

JUST THE FACTS

ACROSS

1. Sir's partner
5. Formal jacket feature
13. Competent
14. Proclaim
15. Night light
16. Reminded an actor of a line, perhaps
17. Almost-last words from Caesar
19. Mascara site
20. Cross words
24. What a slush fund might fund
28. Scarlett O'Hara or Joan of Arc
30. Better ventilated
32. Computer networking device
33. Reason for an 18-DOWN
35. Todd McFarlane comic book character
36. Hankerings
37. "Ready or not, here I _____!"
39. Art technique that combines enamel and metal
44. Wins back
48. _____ Abby, popular advice column
49. Wi-Fi alternative
50. Roosevelt, Wilson, and Hoover
51. Breaks up hurriedly
52. Leave in, to an editor

DOWN

1. Challenge for a barber
2. Aid and _____
3. Frequently
4. Maître d's offering
5. "It's a Wonderful Life" director
6. Torrent
7. One more
8. Heavy reading?
9. Male sheep
10. Kitchen pest
11. Diamonds, slangily
12. _____ Zeppelin
18. Clean up, in a way
20. Progresso product
21. Sandwich bread
22. All over again
23. Beach bird
24. Newborn
25. Anger
26. Clothes presser
27. Life stories, for short
29. Gift on Valentine's Day
31. Lean back
34. Tenant
38. Sprays
39. Links rental
40. "What are the _____?"
41. Straight, at the bar
42. Partner of rank and serial number
43. Formerly, formerly
44. Hi-_____ graphics
45. "Yadda, yadda, yadda"

46. When doubled, a dance
47. Allow

Answers on page 241.

RAISE A GLASS

ACROSS

1. Belgian brews
5. Make-or-break
13. Hooligan
14. Ponder
15. Farm measure
16. Tacked on
17. What TV's Laverne and Shirley brewed up
19. On a deck, perhaps
20. Slam-dance
24. Fab Four drummer
28. Moral consideration
30. Muslim leaders: var.
32. Blowhard's output
33. Went by, as time
35. Aftermath of a lashing
36. "The Way We _____"
37. Pooped
39. Triangular Halloween treat
44. Handel bars
48. Domain
49. Feeling more isolated
50. Caboose
51. Hardly chic
52. Soul mate

DOWN

1. "C'est la vie"
2. Ness, for one
3. Coin with 12 stars on it
4. "Let it stand"
5. Grumbles
6. Delhi money
7. Accuse of misconduct
8. Bleacher feature
9. Bed-and-breakfast
10. Bounder
11. Chowed down
12. Called the shots
18. Ornamental cup holders
20. Remote button
21. Iridescent gem
22. Open, as an envelope
23. His partner
24. Misrepresent
25. Scheherazade specialty
26. Banned apple orchard spray
27. Pickable
29. Obstreperous
31. Amy of "Strangers with Candy"
34. Refuses to admit
38. Be crazy about
39. Pepsi, for one
40. Atkins diet no-no
41. Creme-filled cookie
42. Try for a part
43. _____ a soul
44. Ancient
45. Beluga yield
46. Mandela's org.
47. _____ Aviv

POSITIVELY CHARGED

ACROSS

1. Nuclear particles
8. Chasms
13. Hearing range
14. Dickens's _____ Heep
15. Animal fat
16. Cavern, in poetry
17. Sermon subject
18. Try, as a case
20. 1773 jetsam
21. "I never said half the things I said" sayer
24. Longitude crosser: abbr.
25. Auction action
26. Tangle, as in a net
28. Circuit
31. Rich cake
32. Justification
34. Yellow or Red
35. Last: abbr.
36. Cool event
41. Exxon product
42. Iridescent gem
43. Divinity school subject: abbr.
44. Emasculate
46. Tapioca source
49. Feudal lord
50. They're left behind
51. Perturb
52. Rappers, generically

DOWN

1. Easy _____
2. AM/FM device
3. Rocket gasket: hyph.
4. Kitchen measure: abbr.
5. "So that's it!"
6. Snacked
7. Have the helm
8. Written assurance
9. Big coffee holder
10. Smaller than
11. China setting
12. Encase
19. "_____ you kidding?"
22. Nile bird
23. Chewy, sweet candy owned by Nestle: hyph.
27. Haunted house sound
28. Trendy salad green
29. Skin pigment
30. Some cricketers
33. Brief time out?
34. 1984 Hannah/Hanks comedy
37. Harness racer
38. Boiling mad
39. "When pigs fly!"
40. "Einstein on the Beach" composer Philip
45. "Give it _____!"
47. Hog heaven?
48. Friend of Frodo

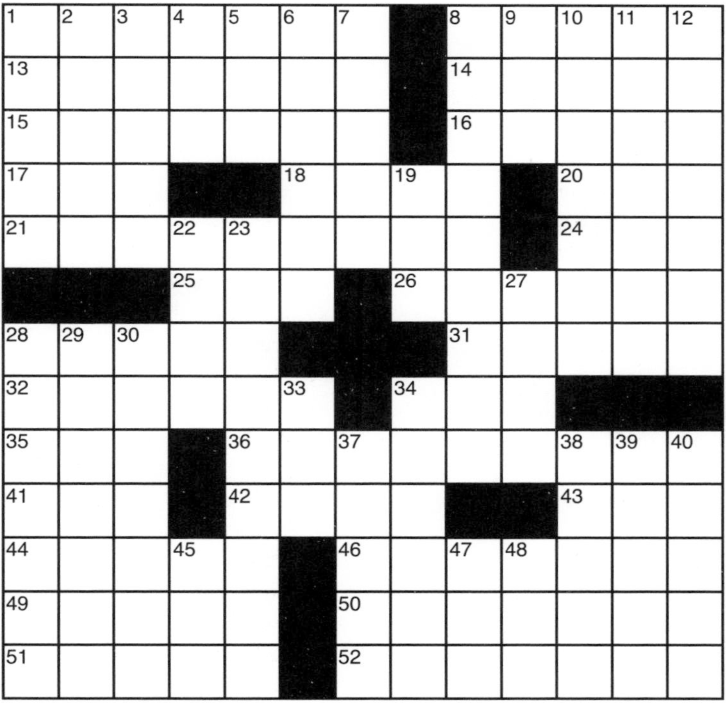

Answers on page 241.

LET'S EAT

ACROSS

1. Puppy food
5. Egyptian snakes
9. Kind of part
12. Actor Jackman of "X-Men"
13. Four Corners state
14. "Oh, there you _____!"
15. Capri, for one
16. Small boat
17. Food container
18. "Scram!" in old slang
20. Superlative
21. Carve
23. One of the 5 W's
27. Barricade
31. Pester
33. Bite-size burger
34. Ballroom dance: hyph.
36. Down at the heels
37. Spanish dish
39. Physics calculation
42. Rears, slangily
47. Lyrical Gershwin
48. Lab vessel
49. Dentist's request
50. Mark of perfection
51. Research facility: abbr.
52. Subcompact
53. Child's play?
54. Awfully long time
55. Aberdeen native

DOWN

1. Fashionable
2. "Pipe down!"
3. Eye up and down
4. "Whoopee!"
5. "The Age of Anxiety" poet
6. Followers of Zeno
7. Social gatherings
8. Like a wallflower
9. Restrain
10. Colored eye part
11. Carnival sight
19. Sonora snooze
20. Misrepresent
22. Dips for chips
23. One of the 5 W's
24. _____ Solo of "Star Wars"
25. "Able was I _____ ..."
26. Talks hoarsely
28. "To Autumn," e.g.
29. Disobeyed a zoo sign?
30. Swelter
32. Part of ISO (personal ad word)
35. "The magic word"
38. Sings lively
39. Baseball glove
40. Atlas stat
41. Warbled
43. _____ of Maine (toothpaste brand)
44. Colossal
45. Gambling mecca
46. Agitated state
48. By means of

Answers on page 241.

COLLEAGUES

ACROSS

1. Wacky
5. Military facility
9. Muscular actor on "The A-Team"
12. Akron's state
13. "Ah, of course"
14. "Gotcha!"
15. Secret company bigwig
18. Pirate's salutation
19. Approving answer
20. Sinister spirit
22. Superpower until 1991: abbr.
25. Figure skating feat
26. Peruvian of yore
27. Political inits.
30. 1943 Ginger Rogers movie
33. Behave
34. Bit of a shock
35. Common disclaimer
36. Unit of heredity
37. Blood category
38. "Magnum, P.I." setting
41. Wise man's herb?
42. Barney Gumble, to Homer Simpson
48. Palooka
49. Package under the Christmas tree
50. It means "billionth"
51. Stat for a slugger
52. Some pens
53. Grand _____

DOWN

1. Cordoba couple
2. Yellowfin tuna
3. Light-bulb thread
4. Initial advantage
5. "Spin _____" (sitcom)
6. Symbol of Egyptian royalty
7. _____ culpa
8. The "p" in WPM
9. "Bulletproof _____" (2003 action film)
10. Demeter's mother
11. Margaret Thatcher, e.g.
16. Smoking alternative
17. Blue Jays, on the scoreboard
20. Type of bank
21. Veep, e.g.
22. Tom or Sam, e.g.
23. Sean Connery, for one
24. Sleuth Spade
26. It has a cord and a board
27. Driver's control
28. Garfield's pal
29. Colombian currency
31. Time of anticipation
32. Futuristic weapons
36. Pistol
37. Indent key
38. Scent
39. Fast horse
40. Player of old tunes
41. Mil. ranks
43. CIA counterpart
44. It's opposite IX on clocks
45. Cowboys' org.

46. Kind of sample
47. _____ Kippur

iSOLVE

ACROSS

1. Tablet computer released by Apple in 2010
5. Pops' pops
13. 2009 movie starring Daniel Day-Lewis as director Guido Contini
14. Fact-finding
15. A couple's night out
16. Short-lived fads
17. Properly arranged
19. Support with stone, as an embankment
20. Many, many moons
21. Skunk's defense
23. "Mangia!"
24. Luau dish
25. Creamsicle color
28. Place of worship
31. Easy gallop
32. Feudal lords
33. Do-it-yourselfer's purchase
34. Place to enter a PIN: abbr.
35. Santa's sackful
37. Boozer
40. Sports figures?
43. Place for a catheter, perhaps
45. Until this time, in a legal document perhaps
47. The "Balloon Boy," e.g.
48. "Yadda yadda yadda"
49. Pot builder
50. Zapped, in a way
51. Garden intruder

DOWN

1. Many an art film
2. Baby grand, e.g.
3. Playwright Chekhov
4. Lots of bucks
5. Most like Midas
6. Not an original
7. Cigarette's end
8. _____-do-well
9. "There Is Nothing Like a _____"
10. Thwart
11. Land
12. Smash to smithereens
18. "Lorna _____"
22. Ice cream flavor with nuts and marshmallows
24. Porky or Babe, e.g.
26. Worker's reward
27. Colony member
28. Horror film character
29. Ancient Syrian
30. Loser's request
36. Unconventional
37. Excelled
38. Declaim
39. Imposed a levy on
41. "Shall I compare _____ to a summer's day?"
42. _____ good example
44. Take out of the freezer
46. No longer working: abbr.

Answers on page 242.

SWEET FOR THE SWEET

ACROSS

1. Nestle-brand nonpareils
8. Happen again
13. One person-boat made with animal hides
14. Ludicrous
15. Connective gizmo
16. Sonnets and such
17. Answer to "Shall we?"
18. Go out after a pass?
20. Holiday _____
21. Pretentious sort
23. Golfer's goal
24. Call to Bo Peep
25. "Ciao!"
27. Tolkien beast
28. High spirits
31. Spring (from)
34. Seek a seat
35. Tennyson poem
37. Asner and O'Neill
38. "The loneliest number"
39. Landscape that may include caverns and sinkholes
43. "Sometimes you feel like a _____ ..."
44. Eye rakishly
46. Barn topper
47. Embarrass
49. An American in Paris?
51. Beneficiary
52. Shoreline problem
53. Chipped in chips
54. Candy that makes your mouth burn

DOWN

1. Massage target, sometimes
2. Junction points
3. Give a speech
4. Word after time or time-release
5. Make a scene?
6. Implored
7. Colorful wrap
8. Its mouth is nowhere near its head
9. Opposite of WSW: abbr.
10. 1974 album by Elton John
11. Disentangle
12. Show, as a historic battle
19. Loiter
22. Not dis
26. Securing, as a bow
28. Site of a 1983 U.S. invasion, also known as the "Island of Spice"
29. Society that's for the birds
30. Coffee choice
32. Lodge member
33. Groveling
36. One who digs deeply
38. _____ and aahed
40. 4:1, e.g.
41. Condescending one
42. Sea swallows
45. Dublin's home
48. "Told ya!"
50. Landscaper's need

Answers on page 242.

THE ART OF FLOWER ARRANGING

ACROSS

1. "Deeper Than the Dead" author Hoag
5. Give a bad time
8. Dance move
12. Pizza cooker
13. Suffix for orange or lemon
14. "See ya," in Salerno
15. Pastel blossom
17. Shrek, for one
18. Thanksgiving tuber
19. Aquafresh competitor
20. Mormon Tabernacle Choir home: abbr.
23. Chessmaster Bobby
26. Slightest
28. Increases to 300% of the original size
31. Cross inscription
32. Route
33. Opera revived by Elton John and Tim Rice
34. Bell sound
36. Wing it
37. Checks who's at the door
39. "_____-haw!"
40. Get squeaky-clean
42. Yellowfin tuna
44. Toledo, Ohio's lake
45. Fragrant and slender purplish flower
50. Love, Latin-style
51. Some people keep it secret
52. Clinton opponent in '96
53. Daly of "Cagney & Lacey"
54. Actress Gretchen
55. Little noise at the dog park

DOWN

1. Bikini part
2. Prefix before "fauna"
3. Word on some doors
4. Like squid spray
5. Supermodel Campbell
6. 30-second spots
7. Expletive heard on "Leave it to Beaver"
8. Grid material included with Yahtzee
9. Showy orange-yellow bloom
10. Spock's feature
11. Whitman or Whittier, e.g.
16. Huck Finn's boat
19. Actor McBride of "Boston Public"
20. Went downhill fast?
21. German director Riefenstahl
22. Bright red fluffy blossom
24. Thespian's locale
25. It may be piercing
27. Instruction under a dotted line
29. Falco of "Nurse Jackie"
30. Kemo _____ (Lone Ranger's nickname)
32. Direction opposite ESE: abbr.
35. British verb ending
36. 1975 Wimbledon winner Arthur
38. "Bolero" composer

40. Tuckered out
41. "Stripes" subject
43. _____ 500 (Memorial Day weekend race)
45. On the _____ (running)

46. "It was 20 years _____ today..."
47. Pseudonym in court cases
48. Right angle-shaped pipe
49. Good name

Answers on page 242.

SEASONAL THEME

ACROSS

1. Skip a turn
5. Try a little of
10. Alaskan islander
12. Big name in aluminum
13. Come-ons
14. Big winds
15. Hare that leaves candy
17. Atlanta-to-Tampa dir.
18. "_____ lookin' at ya"
19. Bonnie's partner
21. Forty-niner's filing
23. Small battery size
26. They're often found at Easter
29. Allow in
30. Diarist Nin
31. River through Paris
32. Boxer's dream
33. Frisky swimmer
34. Active ingredient in Off!

DOWN

1. Loses color
2. "John Doe"
3. Taste or touch
4. Treat for winter birds
5. Like many manila folders
6. Appeal
7. Tea cake
8. Whistle-stops
9. Requiring no great labor
11. Lao-_____
16. Cat and hat, e.g.
19. Incisor neighbor
20. Seat on shafts
21. West Pointer
22. Word after speed or age
23. Kind of marble
24. Like a gymnast
25. Desirable quality
26. El _____, Texas
27. "Can't Help Lovin' _____ Man" ("Show Boat" song)
28. Oklahoma city

Answers on page 242.

FEMALE FINISHERS

ACROSS

1. Stadium level
5. Resistance unit
8. Hissy fit
12. Gumbo veggie
13. Besmirch
14. Protagonist
15. Mythical half-human sex creatures
17. Absent
18. Cambridge University: abbr.
19. Middle school: abbr.
20. Errand boy
23. Honeycomb material
27. Very dry
28. Finishes donning a dress, say
29. Be in debt to
30. Knight's title
31. Sire
32. "… needs a _____ like a fish needs a bicycle"
33. "Nova" network
34. Woodwind instrument
35. Goose egg
36. Doesn't play this round
38. Crisp (but easily wrinkled) fabric
39. Set on fire
40. Omelet utensil
41. October gem
43. 2005 Steve Martin/Claire Danes movie
48. Queen of Sparta
49. What you do if you don't know the words

50. Buffalo's lake
51. Calendar units
52. "Uh-huh!"
53. New band's submission

DOWN

1. Actor Hanks
2. "I like _____" ('50s political slogan)
3. Go astray
4. Butted
5. Pass over
6. Hoodwinked
7. "_____ Doubtfire"
8. Erstwhile Persian rulers
9. Katie Couric and Diane Sawyer, e.g.
10. Writer Levin
11. Plaything
16. Lung filler
19. Joke
20. Pants and heaves
21. Pygmy antelope
22. From 2009–2017, Michelle Obama
23. Racist
24. Fencing sword
25. Conscious
26. Inert gas
28. Domestic ox from India
31. Ugg product
35. Criticized sharply
37. "_____ Marner"
38. Track circuit
40. "_____ and Circumstance"
41. Timeworn

42. Little legume
43. Timid
44. Shade of color

45. Wrath
46. Periphery
47. August sign

1	2	3	4		5	6	7		8	9	10	11
12					13				14			
15				16					17			
			18						19			
20	21	22				23	24				25	26
27					28					29		
30				31						32		
33				34					35			
36			37					38				
		39					40					
41	42				43	44				45	46	47
48					49				50			
51					52				53			

SEXIEST MAN ALIVE

ACROSS

1. Biblical flood survivor
5. A long way away
9. Office dupes, for short
12. _____ in a blue moon
13. Sub station?
14. Motor add-on
15. Land bordered by the Mekong
16. 2003 & 2009
17. Me, to Miss Piggy
18. Angry rant
20. 1986
22. Bird with a white tail
23. Sarah McLachlan hit of 1998
25. Polly, to Tom Sawyer
26. Wks. and wks.
27. _____ Park, Colorado
28. 2005
32. Sing softly
33. Lee, director of "Taking Wood-stock"
34. Sergeant or corporal, e.g.
35. *Cuatro* doubled
36. Financial daily, initially
39. About to bat
41. Split down the middle
43. Land west of Eng.
44. Chow _____
46. Short race, for short
47. _____ Elton John
48. Cut _____ (boogie)
49. _____ Cobb of "12 Angry Men"
50. Tarzan portrayer Ron
51. One of nine for a nonagon
52. Star sci.

DOWN

1. 1992
2. Walking _____ (elated)
3. Snack for a squirrel
4. "For _____ jolly good fel-low..."
5. Expanded a building
6. Finder's _____
7. First Greek letter
8. Kelly of "Live with Regis and Kelly"
9. Morning or afternoon travel
10. 1997 & 2006
11. Peter, Paul, and Mary
19. 2007
21. Dermatologist's concern
24. Soul singer Hayes
27. Urge into action
28. Spring VIP in an all-male calendar
29. 1989
30. "I'd like to buy the world a _____ . . ."
31. Send over the edge
32. 1990
35. Actress Cheri of "Scary Movie"
36. Lessens in intensity
37. Hard rain?
38. 1988: abbr.
40. Dec. holiday
42. Granada greeting
45. Birth control option, briefly

Answers on page 242.

HEROINES OF HISTORY

ACROSS

1. Dispensed candy
4. Manicurist's tool
8. Ralph Lauren brand
12. Get older
13. Above
14. Hawaiian feast
15. Bikini piece
16. Civil rights pioneer
18. _____ pressure
20. Beginning
21. Noted flag maker
24. Earmark
25. Have lunch
26. UK leaders, for short
29. Enter
30. Drive up the wall
31. Kind of massage
32. Hold the deed to
33. Lingerie store item
34. Oscar or Tony
35. "The Maid of Orleans"
37. "The Private Lives of Elizabeth and _____" (1939 film)
40. Actress Rinna
41. America's first woman in space
44. Incorrect
47. Like a wanted G.I.
48. Satanic
49. "Entourage" network
50. Word in the Golden Rule
51. Serve supper to
52. Number of pool pockets

DOWN

1. Butter serving
2. Simon Cowell has a large one
3. German airship
4. Sherwood _____
5. Piano key material
6. French article
7. Historical time
8. Architectural drawings
9. Yours and mine
10. Canoeing site
11. Evict
17. Blog entry
19. School attended by Prince William
21. _____-dryer
22. Showed again
23. Tree symbolizing strength
24. A while _____
26. Ancient Egyptian rulers
27. Fashion designer Jacobs
28. Sex Pistols bassist Vicious
30. Saver's holding, briefly
31. Holiday poem opener
33. Like economy cars, say
34. Off the beaten path
35. Dessert with a hyphen in its name
36. _____ but a goodie
37. Biblical man conned out of birthright
38. Like logs
39. One-armed bandit
42. "The Marriage _____" (reality show)

43. "Now _____ heard everything!"
45. Seeley Booth's employer on "Bones": abbr.
46. "Family Guy" network

1	2	3		4	5	6	7		8	9	10	11
12				13					14			
15				16				17				
		18	19					20				
	21					22	23					
24						25				26	27	28
29					30				31			
32				33				34				
			35				36					
37	38	39					40					
41					42	43				44	45	46
47					48				49			
50					51				52			

SUPERMODELS

ACROSS

1. "_____ später" (German farewell)
4. Persona non _____
9. Frequently, to poets
12. Taylor of fashion
13. Irritates
14. Yea's opposite
15. Supermodel with the fragrance Cat Deluxe
18. Well-timed
19. Move gingerly
20. Air Jordans
21. eBay user
23. Ginger _____
24. Play for doughs
26. Supermodel once married to John Mellencamp
31. Tennis milieu
32. Use scissors
34. Prickly plant
37. Type of lipstick
39. Herbal healer
40. Expand
42. Supermodel on the cover of the first issue of "George"
45. _____ Haw
46. Pulitzer-winning play "August _____ County"
47. Sharp intelligence
48. Widths of some spaces: abbr.
49. Helmeted worker
50. Military authority: abbr.

DOWN

1. Potassium source
2. Heaped up
3. Swimming apparatus
4. Handlebar attachments
5. Puerto _____
6. "Oh, woe!"
7. Pro follower
8. Egyptian headdress symbol
9. Ryan of "Love Story"
10. Like some eyelashes
11. Steven of Aerosmith
16. One of the Three Stooges
17. Underneath
21. Saliva
22. Screw up
24. Lions' prey
25. Poetic contraction
27. Performed in a play
28. Letters for debtors
29. Chill, as beer in a cooler
30. Expressed by digits
33. Look after
34. Hidden supply
35. Alexander McQueen's _____ shoes
36. Frozen yogurt holders
37. Show fear
38. Battle of Britain org.
40. Muffin content
41. Fashion or passion
43. _____ Kippur
44. Bruckheimer's CBS TV franchise

Answers on page 243.

LIPSTICK

ACROSS

1. Major or Minor
5. Effects used in "Avatar": abbr.
8. Baby's first word, perhaps
12. Spiritual leader
13. State tree of Iowa
14. Insulated boots
15. Red by MAC
18. Buffoon
19. "_____ Hop" (1958 #1 hit)
20. Red by CoverGirl
25. Not urban
26. Last name in ice cream
27. Votes for passage
28. Arthur of "The Golden Girls"
29. Heidi's hubby
33. Designer Claiborne
34. In the lead
35. Red by L'Oreal
40. _____ Walker (Whiskey brand)
41. Flexible wood
42. Red by Revlon
48. Zeno's home
49. "But what _____ know?"
50. _____ tea
51. Those in Tlaquepaque
52. "Hang on a _____!"
53. Last letter in a phonetic alphabet

DOWN

1. It's said to go before beauty
2. Chevy Blazer, for one
3. Intense anger
4. Night lights
5. Snug as a bug in a rug
6. Yak
7. Eisenhower's nickname
8. Prefix with task or millionaire
9. Supreme Court justice appointed by George W. Bush
10. Chinese dish
11. Fireplace residue
16. Title character played by Jason Lee
17. Doilyish
20. Bawl
21. Shade of color
22. It's shorter than an eon
23. Former talk show host Gibbons
24. Boise's state: abbr.
28. Pen or lighter brand
29. The entertainment industry, slangily
30. Suffix with racket or auction
31. Tow grp.
32. The "bad" cholesterol: abbr.
33. Arm or leg, e.g.
34. _____-deucey (dice game)
35. Number of Blind Mice
36. Iranian coins
37. "Nor care for wind, or tide, _____" (John Burroughs)
38. Dads
39. Line from a song
43. Newspaper VIPs
44. _____ v. Wade
45. Post-op patient's locale

46. _____ Aviv
47. End of many university
     domain names

1	2	3	4		5	6	7		8	9	10	11
12					13				14			
15				16				17				
			18					19				
20	21	22				23	24					
25						26						
27						28				29	30	31	32
				33				34			
35	36	37	38				39				
40							41				
42					43	44				45	46	47
48					49				50			
51					52				53			

Answers on page 243.

PARENT COMPANY

ACROSS

1. Archipelago unit: abbr.
4. Some bout outcomes, briefly
8. Last section of a London phone book
12. Comb maker
13. Westheimer of sex ed
14. "Haven't _____ you somewhere before?"
15. 1948 Irene Dunne film
18. Creedence Clearwater Revival hit of 1968
19. Nastier
20. Kentucky Derby time
21. Strike callers
23. Off-road transport: abbr.
24. On _____ with (equal to)
26. First name in beauty
28. 1986 Sissy Spacek/Anne Bancroft film
31. Sotomayor on the Supreme Court
32. Guesstimate words
33. And the like: abbr.
34. _____ pump
36. Stun
39. Brick houses
41. Spotted animals
44. 1981 Faye Dunaway film
46. All over again
47. *E pluribus* _____
48. Bolted down some nuts?
49. Loch _____ monster
50. Make the grade?
51. Tennis judge's cry

DOWN

1. Hieroglyphics bird
2. Truth _____
3. Gibbons of TV
4. Spot to spot dates
5. Small, oval-shaped fruit
6. Gambling spot: abbr.
7. A Stooge
8. Malt beverage introduced in 1993
9. Flow (from)
10. Greek goddess of grain and fertility
11. "Feed a cold, _____ a fever"
16. Oscar-nominated role for Morita
17. Changes hands?
22. 1983 Teri Garr film
25. First stage
27. Bridal party
28. In progress
29. Workers make them
30. He went to Hades to rescue Eurydice
31. Deck figure
35. Exhaust, as supplies
37. NBA Rookie of the Year in 1993
38. "_____ not, want not"
40. Some luxury cars
42. Southern roots
43. Editor's "leave it alone"
45. "CSI" evidence

Answers on page 243.

SONGS FROM THE HEART

ACROSS

1. Exclamation from Homer
4. Fairy tale creature
7. Miles off
11. Let go
13. Top of a clock dial
14. Opening for a dermatologist
15. Deal with impatiently, as mail
17. Bit of a drag
18. The Beatles, 1964
20. "_____ Liaisons Dangere-uses"
21. Backing for an exhibit?
24. Air Supply, 1980
28. "What _____, chopped liver?"
29. Father, for short
30. Writer Wolitzer
31. Elvis Presley, 1956
36. "Gladiator" setting
37. Pooh's pal
38. Rodgers and Hammerstein, 1945
44. Next-to-last Golden Rule word
46. Follow too closely
47. Julia of "The Addams Family"
48. Hip-hop's Dr. _____
49. Eliza's 'elper in "My Fair Lady"
50. Lt. Kojak's employer
51. Opposite of NNE
52. Natural _____

DOWN

1. Raw material?
2. Farm team
3. _____ & Shoulders
4. Photographic term
5. Schreiber of "The Manchurian Candidate"
6. Better than good
7. Take to a higher court
8. Alcott's "Little Women," e.g.
9. Speak like a Peke
10. Ring leader?, for short
12. It turns a bit
16. Sub in a tub
19. Playboy Hugh, familiarly
22. Next-to-last fairy tale word
23. Journey part
24. Another name for Cupid
25. Paint the town red
26. Hanoi festival
27. Wrap-up
28. Carte start
32. Wrap up
33. _____ tai
34. Winter air
35. Word before ball or City
39. British Incs.
40. Boating blades
41. Yin's counterpart
42. Other, in España
43. 180° turns, slangily
44. Ode subject
45. House call?

Answers on page 243.

MEMORABLE FEMALE ROLES

ACROSS

1. _____ support (over-the-phone service)
5. Boxing moves
9. "House" actor Penn
12. About 30% of the Earth's land
13. Tony's "Village Voice" awards counterpart
14. Org. whose logo displays an eagle holding two guns: abbr.
15. Memorable role in "A Streetcar Named Desire"
18. "_____ Sleep in the Subway" (Petula Clark hit)
19. Battle sides?
20. Fitness system started by Billy Blanks
23. Suffix meaning "sugar"
24. Memorable role in "Casablanca"
27. Computer data storage capacity: abbr.
30. Smeltery refuse
31. Creative, warm-hearted individual, it's said
32. Naked
33. Home to the Sun Devils: abbr.
34. Memorable title role for Sally Field
36. Ovine opinion
38. Insecure feeling
39. Rice _____: side dish
42. Utters
44. Memorable role in "Gone With the Wind"
49. So far
50. Chemistry class model
51. Stuntman Knievel
52. Ruby or Sandra
53. Bugle call at a military funeral
54. Roadside diner sign

DOWN

1. Soft drink, or part of the can it comes in
2. US immigrant's class: abbr.
3. Govt. group with a Director: abbr.
4. Gucci collectible
5. "Crocodile Rock" singer Elton
6. Drive the getaway car, e.g.
7. Auction offer
8. Dr. who introduced The Lorax
9. Fort with a lot of gold
10. R&B singer India._____
11. Scottish girl
16. "Awesome!"
17. Striped stinger
20. "_____ far, far better thing . . ."
21. "_____ fair in love and war"
22. Jacob's biblical twin
23. Scratch-n-sniff emanation
25. Bone that touches the humerus
26. Keanu, in "The Matrix"

27. Helgenberger of "CSI"
28. Disco and Swing, for two
29. Get together
32. Wailing spirit, in Gaelic folklore
35. It's sometimes held in delis
36. Karaoke joint, usually
37. Note that sounds the same as G#
39. Doctoral degree for a therapist

40. Slurpee competitor
41. Tardy
42. Cop's request to a bad guy
43. They may be drive-up: abbr.
45. In-flight stat
46. Frank Sinatra ex Gardner
47. Out of the mil.
48. Franken and Sharpton, for two

 Answers on page 243.

WHOSE SHOES?

ACROSS

1. Break into computer files
5. Therapeutic getaway
8. River through Russia
12. Work safety agency: abbr.
13. It goes away when you stand
14. "Happy birthday _____ ..."
15. Strappy footwear
18. Prefix for "dermis"
19. Be in arrears
20. Get rid of
21. Succumb to gravity
23. Actor McKellen
24. Narrow tubular pasta
26. "For Those About to Rock (We Salute You)" band
28. Cuppa contents, to a Brit
31. Spiky footwear
34. "The dog _____ my homework"
35. Puts on TV
36. Haphazard way to run
37. Dadaist painter Jean
38. Trophy
39. Figure in a skating rink?
42. "Burn Notice" network
44. Independence Day mo.
47. Long footwear
50. Sicilian spewer
51. "The Greatest"
52. Lender bought by Bank of America in 2005: abbr.
53. Winter ride
54. "Lock U Down" R&B singer
55. In _____ (all packaged together)

DOWN

1. Where the heart is, it's said
2. Pronto: abbr.
3. Mystery writer Agatha
4. Former senator _____ Bailey Hutchison
5. Cole _____
6. Window unit
7. Donkey Kong, for one
8. Illegal maneuver on many roads: hyph.
9. Actress Downey
10. Guitarist's boxes
11. _____-majeste
16. Go running in the park, e.g.
17. Fruit in a "Melba" dessert
22. Feel sick
23. Vows at the altar
24. When doubled, a Gabor sister
25. Wednesday Addams's cousin
26. "Take _____ from me ..."
27. Midpoint: abbr.
28. Staff postings for the short term
29. "Hold on Tight" prog-rock band: abbr.
30. Pose a question
32. It gets its own day in April
33. Perrier, par exemple
37. Up next
38. Subway alternative
39. _____ out a living
40. On a global scale: abbr.
41. KISS frontman Simmons

42. Like some Americans abroad, it's said
43. Actor LaBeouf
45. "Reader" on the newsstands

46. Aspiring lawyer's test: abbr.
48. "_____ Spartacus!"
49. Medical suffix

1	2	3	4		5	6	7		8	9	10	11
12					13				14			
15				16				17				
18				19				20				
		21	22				23					
24	25				26	27				28	29	30
31				32				33				
34				35				36				
			37					38				
39	40	41				42	43			44	45	46
47				48				49				
50				51				52				
53				54				55				

HAIR THROUGHOUT THE DECADES

ACROSS

1. First female Speaker of the House Nancy
7. "Pride and Prejudice" author Jane
13. Things you order everyday, e.g.
14. Wicked
15. With "The," popular hairstyle of the 1990s
16. Gives the evil eye
17. Israeli political party for Benjamin Netanyahu
18. Popular hairstyle of the 1950s/1960s
19. Legumes used as a "gum" in thickening agents
21. It's shaped like a right angle when uppercase
25. Awesome
30. Popular hairstyle of the 1970s
31. Popular hairstyle of the 1920s
33. Popular hairstyle of the 1980s
34. Female breakdancing participant, slangily: hyph.
36. Live-in childcare specialists
38. "Sleeping with the _____" (Julia Roberts movie)
40. Popular hairstyle of the 1960s
44. Makes it through
49. Italian eatery at the mall
50. Popular hairstyle (in punk circles) in the 1980s
51. "Miss _____" (musical based on "Madame Butterfly")
52. Sickle-cell affliction
53. Eagle's grabbers
54. "The Sixth Sense" star Haley Joel _____

DOWN

1. Knitting maneuver
2. Morales of "La Bamba"
3. "_____ be a lady tonight . . ."
4. Honolulu's island
5. Heavy hammer
6. Speck on a globe: abbr.
7. Tool used for boring holes
8. Except
9. Iranian ruler, until 1979
10. "Cornflake Girl" singer Amos
11. Abbr. on a mountain sign
12. Financial page inits.
18. Hogwash
20. City, informally
21. Mad scientist's hangout
22. D followers
23. Prefix meaning "three"
24. Craggy peak
26. Network that was subsumed into The CW
27. Louvre Pyramid architect I.M.
28. Before, to a poet
29. Abbr. in an apartment ad
32. Word Emeril Lagasse says a lot

35. Cleveland Cavaliers star
    _____ James
37. Hosiery purchase
39. Twelve o'clock times
40. "Hey...over here!" noise
41. Quatrain rhyme scheme,
    maybe
42. Author Sheehy

43. "*Cogito, _____ sum*"
45. "Excuse me...I was here
    first" noise
46. Identical
47. One may be identical
48. Three-handed card game
50. Cultural Revolution leader

1	2	3	4	5	6		7	8	9	10	11	12
13							14					
15							16					
17						18						
			19	20								
21	22	23	24					25	26	27	28	29
30					31		32		33			
34			35		36		37					
			38	39								
40	41	42	43					44	45	46	47	48
49							50					
51							52					
53							54					

Answers on page 244.

SHOP 'TIL YOU DROP

ACROSS

1. "Like, run, _____!" (request frequently made by Shaggy in cartoons)
6. Spacy-sounding Toyota Camry variety
12. Part of some African vacations
14. Like some salons or restrooms
15. Event that a 30-ACROSS is likely to find
17. Lithuania until 1991, e.g.: abbr.
18. Thor Heyerdahl's "_____-Tiki"
19. Word after bake or garage
20. Jeans fabrics
23. Constellation with a belt
26. Letters after N
27. "Ghost Whisperer" network
30. Expert shopper
33. Tattoos, slangily
34. Country lanes: abbr.
35. It's located just above the heart
36. Creating
38. Cruise once nicknamed "TomKitten" by the media
42. South Bend's state: abbr.
43. Reason to stop on a road trip
46. Location that 30-ACROSS is likely to check out
50. "Twenty Questions" category
51. Coronary or pulmonary, for instance
52. Fruit rich in potassium
53. Tennis star Monica

DOWN

1. Fast NY-to-Paris jets, once: abbr.
2. Crow noises
3. "_____ a life of Sensations rather than of Thoughts!" (John Keats)
4. Klutzy person
5. It usually requires a cast to keep the elbow immobile
6. Major London tabloid
7. "The loneliest number"
8. Where eye shadow is applied
9. Out in the ocean
10. Flesh and blood
11. One of two bars on a car
13. Do some laundry work
16. Lightweight paper used for tracing
20. Shih Tzu, e.g.
21. Abbr. on a speed limit sign
22. Wastes an opportunity
23. Kimono sash
24. Sought office
25. Bug the heck out of
27. Midpoint: abbr.
28. Roulette table action
29. Mrs., in Managua: abbr.
31. Ore-_____ (Tater Tots brand)
32. Yuletide quaff

37. Ancient Machu Picchu dweller
38. Scrape reminder
39. Radius neighbor
40. One way to hold your horses
41. "_____ Rock" (Simon and Garfunkel song)

43. "The Science of Sleep" actor _____ Garcia Bernal
44. Small farm size
45. "The _____ the limit!"
47. Bled in the wash
48. Pie _____ mode
49. Hwy., for one: abbr.

1	2	3	4	5		6	7	8	9	10	11
12					13		14				
15						16					
17				18					19		
			20				21	22			
23	24	25				26				27	28	29
30				31				32			
33				34				35			
			36			37					
38	39	40	41			42				43	44	45
46				47	48				49		
50							51				
52								53			

Answers on page 244.

ACROSS

1. Helper: abbr.
5. 5-digit number on an envelope: abbr.
8. Get the question wrong
12. Film _____ (detective genre)
13. Greek vowel
14. _____-Day vitamins: hyph.
15. Type of hernia suffered much more by men than by women
17. Like some textbooks
18. Went for the gold?
19. Spray bottle output
21. Boxes that come out during the summer: abbr.
22. "Now I get it" noises
25. Birthstone in a shell
28. Nighttime condition that more men suffer the effects of than women
30. Ark captain
33. Cheer at old-timey football games
34. They require cards and PINs
35. Men are more likely to be of this visual condition than women
38. Encrypted
39. _____-pitch softball
40. Dictator Amin
43. Jacob's biblical twin
45. Delivery doctor, for short: abbr.
47. Prefix before "potent" or "present"
49. Problem way more prevalent in men than in women
52. "Puttin' on the _____" (Taco's only hit)
53. Toronto's province: abbr.
54. Stub _____
55. 2009 show set at William McKinley High School
56. Cloche, for one
57. "Critique of Pure Reason" philosopher Immanuel

DOWN

1. Inner self, to Jung
2. Hedgehog of Sega fame
3. M. Night Shyamalan movie with Mel Gibson
4. Test answer with a $^{50}/_{50}$ shot
5. Type of garden with rocks
6. "Give _____ whirl"
7. It may be read by fortune tellers
8. Site where you get your clicks?
9. Like some coffee
10. "What did I tell you?"
11. Lamentable
16. Word associated with Clay Aiken and Adam Lambert
20. Bitter microbrew choice: abbr.
23. Ginseng or parsley, e.g.
24. Closes an envelope
26. "Everybody Hurts" band
27. Vegas airport code

28. Clothing measurement on a different scale than with men
29. Dr. with his own daytime show
30. Letters on the starship *Enterprise*
31. Winning tic-tac-toe line
32. Pasta firmness request
36. Abbr. on a food label
37. Jordan's Queen _____
40. "_____ Name" (1973 Jim Croce album)
41. UK-based vacuum cleaner company

42. Section for Hawaii or Alaska on a map
44. "That wasn't supposed to happen": hyph.
46. Coca-Cola _____ (failed coffee-flavored soft drink of 2006)
47. Possible URL ending...
48. ...and another possible URL ending
50. Comedian Gasteyer of "Saturday Night Live"
51. "Addams Family" cousin

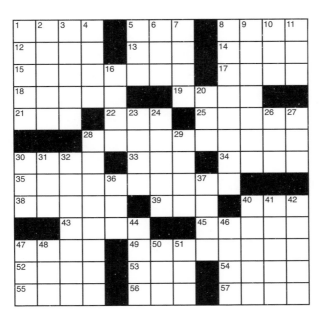

Answers on page 244.

ANTI-WHAT?

ACROSS

1. "Seven whole grains on a mission" cereal
6. Tiresome
9. J. Edgar Hoover's agency: abbr.
12. Principle of consciousness
13. Whaling weapon
15. Anti- on sunglasses
16. Anti- in some vitamins
17. Not-quite-square shape: abbr.
19. Esteem
20. One, in French
22. "It's _____ to the finish!"
25. Ukraine, once: abbr.
26. Anti- in hygiene products
29. Time between two zodiac signs
30. Beach ball filler
31. Bumbling dudes
35. Anti- in some makeup products and medicines
38. Prof's helpers: abbr.
41. "Grumpy Old Men" actor Davis
42. Beef _____-tip
43. Top floor
45. Notable time periods
47. Anti- in some clothing
50. Anti- in some skin care products
53. Change for a quarter
54. Actress Witherspoon of "Four Christmases"
55. Talk nonstop
56. Lightly vandalizes a front yard, perhaps: abbr.
57. Do the Pied Piper's job

DOWN

1. Frat party container
2. U.S.-to-U.K. crossing: abbr.
3. They have some for everyone
4. Put on the payroll
5. Polar covering
6. "So that's what you're up to!"
7. Not strict
8. Headed for a goal
9. Young horses
10. Paycheck extra
11. Prefix before "net" or "national"
14. BlackBerry, e.g: abbr.
18. They're covered by court reporters
20. Bar code: abbr.
21. New, in Nuremburg: Ger.
23. First sign of the zodiac
24. 1976 Sissy Spacek horror movie
27. Place to get a massage and meal
28. Dactyl
32. Less likely to sit still
33. Tree in a Christmas tree lot
34. Poli _____ (college field of study)
36. Keepsake with a picture
37. Actor Depardieu

38. Light blondish
39. Heart chambers
40. Adhere
44. Calligraphy need
46. "A Death in the Family" playwright James

48. Business type popular among lawyers and accountants: abbr.
49. Slalom curve
51. Codebreaking govt. org.
52. Receive

1	2	3	4	5		6	7	8		9	10	11
12						13			14			
15						16						
		17			18		19					
20	21			22		23	24			25		
26			27						28			
29					30				31	32	33	34
			35	36				37				
38	39	40		41						42		
43			44				45		46			
47				48	49		50			51	52
53							54					
55				56				57				

109   Answers on page 244.

FEETS DON'T FAIL ME NOW

ACROSS

1. School stat.
4. Aptitude
9. Sheep peep
12. Big name in makeup
13. "The Transmission Experts"
14. "% Daily Value" precursor
15. Leaves without permission
17. "*Ich bin _____ Berliner*" (JFK quote)
18. Digs out weeds
19. Stunned
20. Scoops water
22. Gets blocked
25. .com alternative
26. "Funny Girl" Fanny
27. Fatal weaknesses
33. Rising sharply
34. 12, in old Rome
35. Starts, as a laptop
38. Acclaims
40. Yours and mine
41. Shopping transport
42. Muslim branch, with "shi"
43. Lifts weights
48. "Attack!" (to a dog)
49. "Save me _____!"
50. The loneliest number
51. "A cockroach!"
52. Thick
53. "Amazing!"

DOWN

1. Baseball execs.
2. Egg fryer
3. A pair of deuces beats it
4. Charlatans
5. Young girl
6. "I love," to Ovid
7. ER venue
8. Wither
9. Bar orders
10. "*Arrivederci!*"
11. 1961 John Updike story set in a grocery store
16. Internet provider: abbr.
19. "A Death in the Family" author
20. Accessory for Mae West or Miss Piggy
21. Curve
22. Advance gradually
23. Speech impediment
24. "And," in Swedish
26. "*Sacre _____!*"
28. Adherents' ending
29. "M*A*S*H" ranks: abbr.
30. Plane seating specification
31. "Diamond _____"
32. "Boom-bah" lead-in
35. A state capital
36. Belly button type
37. Big name in vacuums
38. Axiomatic waste maker
39. "All Things Considered" reporter Shapiro
41. Tax experts
43. Reinforce
44. Take advantage of
45. "12 Angry _____"
46. Lennon's Yoko

47. "Brave _____ World"

Answers on page 244.

DOUBLE YOUR PLEASURE

ACROSS

1. Cram into the overhead
5. What a Breathalyzer measures: abbr.
8. Wolverine, for example (Marvel Comics)
12. "Damn Yankees" femme fatale
13. "From _____ Zinc"
14. Tic-tac-toe choice
15. Start of a quote from Coco Chanel
18. "_____ Helsing" (2004 Hugh Jackman movie)
19. Anglo-Saxon governors
20. Adult education course, often: abbr.
21. Cadenza player
23. Movie gun, for example
26. Quote, part 2
27. Go for a swim, with "take"
31. Scholarship criterion
33. Lists of corrected errors
34. Quote, part 3
36. Quote, part 4
37. "*Comprende*?"
38. Prefix fur inside
40. Accelerator pedal
41. End of the quote
44. "Beetle Bailey" bulldog
45. "Invasion of the Body Snatchers" container
46. Alma mater of Jimmy Carter: abbr.
48. "Dogs"
49. "*Ceci n'est pas ___ pipe*" (inscription on René Magritte's "The Treachery of Images")
50. Fantastic Four co-creater Lee
51. Affixes
52. "_____ your request"
53. 48 in a cup: abbr.

DOWN

1. A Belgradian
2. "Animal House" attire
3. "Alias" actress Lena
4. "All's fair" in it
5. Black rock
6. For each one
7. "Gangsta's Paradise" Grammy-winner
8. Huge shirt size
9. "Ugly Betty" magazine
10. Buy-and-sell pros: abbr.
11. Christmas tune
16. "Anna Karenina" author Tolstoy
17. 100 member political group: abbr.
21. "Doctor's" job
22. "American Pie" actress Reid
23. Acct. credits
24. Prepared leftovers
25. Got adjusted
28. Grosses out
29. "Child's play!"
30. Buys
32. "At last, the weekend!"

33. Israel airline
35. Buy as soon as available
36. Even more tasteless
39. Chophouse order

42. "i" toppers
43. Banish
44. "Death _____ Salesman"
47. Response: abbr.

1	2	3	4		5	6	7		8	9	10	11
12					13				14			
15				16			17					
18				19						20		
			21						22			
23	24	25			26				27	28	29	30
31				32			33					
34					35		36					
37				38		39				40		
	41		42						43			
44					45				46			47
48					49				50			
51					52				53			

Answers on page 245.

GIRLS' NIGHT OUT

ACROSS

1. Fishing spots in Fife
6. "Finger-lickin' good" restaurant
9. Toni Morrison's "_____ Baby"
12. Moving van
13. Salt, to chemists
14. Brian of Roxy Music
15. Girls night out, drink orders #1
18. "Moby-Dick" captain
19. "Paradise City" rocker Rose
20. "_____, poor Yorick!"
21. News initials
23. "Touched by an Angel" costar Della
24. Girls night out, drink order #2
29. Baseball's "Master Melvin"
30. "How to Succeed in Business Without Really Trying" librettist Burrows
31. Whispered story
32. After taxes
33. Thompson of "Back to the Future"
34. Girls night out, drink order #3
36. Certain Gillette razors
38. Bank offering, for short
39. Islamic leader
40. Sunscreen measure: abbr.
42. Turn craft
46. Girls night out, drink order #4

49. Big picture?: abbr.
50. Bullfighter cry
51. Anouk of "La Dolce Vita"
52. _____-Foy, Que.
53. "Awesome!"
54. Back, on a boat

DOWN

1. "The Godfather" enforcer _____ Brasi
2. "Oops!"
3. Home, in Spanish
4. "Nonsense!"
5. _____gin
6. Famous fort
7. Genesis event, with "the"
8. Other Windy City nickname, with "Town"
9. "Fun with Dick and Jane" costar
10. "Nana" star
11. Pre-Raphaelite painter-poet
16. "Grab a partner"
17. _____ Bo
22. Belgrade coins
23. Harder to find
24. Feelings of discomfort
25. Criminal encouragement
26. Bar at the back of a car
27. Babysitter's handful
28. "L'chaim," literally
35. "Here!"
37. "Yo te _____"
40. 1944 E.T.O. battleground
41. "That was a close one!"
43. Point out

44. "Happy Birthday" writer
45. Accordingly
47. "_____ what?"
48. _____-relief

Answers on page 245.

POET'S MUSE

ACROSS
1. "_____ Old House"
5. Short-distance radio user
9. Kind of ribs
12. Litter member
13. Baldwin of "30 Rock"
14. A foot wide?
15. "Are not!" rejoinder
16. Engine sound
17. "The Simpsons" neighbor
18. 2001 hit movie musical
21. Spin doctor
22. Barley sprouts
25. Initial reaction
29. Irish dance
32. Victorian, for one
33. Losing line in tic-tac-toe
34. Cabin locale
39. "Is that clear?"
40. Broods
44. Curry favor with
48. Capt.'s superior
50. Can't stomach
51. Lhasa _____
52. Outside, with "skeleton"
53. Poet Pound
54. Tidy
55. Center of a ball?: abbr.
56. Monday–Sunday
57. Prohibitionists

DOWN
1. Bum
2. Groucho Marx's trade
3. "Briefly…"
4. Minnesota Lutheran college
5. _____ Crunch cereal
6. Cloud
7. Architect Saarinen
8. "Keep on Truckin'" artist
9. European alliance since 1948
10. Drone, e.g.
11. End of a demonstration?
19. Kamoze of reggae
20. Lady, informally
23. Asian chicken general
24. HBO competitor
26. Bill of Rights subject: abbr.
27. Mr. in Iraq
28. "The Joy Luck Club" author Amy
29. Nudge
30. Rocks, in a drink
31. "Earn a paycheck!"
35. Increase, with "up"
36. Brother's boy
37. Indie music genre
38. "The Dark Tower" protagonist
41. Wrestler Roddy
42. English exam finale, often
43. Immunizations
45. Idle
46. French "to be"
47. Highest point
48. Hospital student: abbr.
49. Can

Answers on page 245.

GIRL TALK

ACROSS

1. "Look in the sky! _____ a bird..."
4. Broadcast
8. Geeky, hyper type
12. Disappeared: abbr.
13. "Whadja say?"
14. Aesop's also-ran
15. "_____ and the City" (theme of this puzzle)
16. Beginner's painting class
17. "Enterprise" journey
18. Actress who played Edna Garrett on "The Facts of Life"
21. A play might be seen better with this
22. "Dig in!"
23. Doctrine often read on "Law and Order"
27. Hospital employee: abbr.
28. "Golden" time
29. 112.5-degrees from W
32. "Touch Me" singer
37. California fort
38. "It's of no _____ me"
39. "Return of the Jedi" star
44. Way out
45. Bag of chips, maybe
46. Arthur of "The Golden Girls"
48. Stew jar
49. "*L'Homme*" upstairs?
50. Boy, informally
51. Appreciates
52. Leak slowly

53. "10538 Overture" band

DOWN

1. "Talks" on the computer, for short
2. Business wear accessory
3. Brass band pieces
4. "The Osbournes" mom
5. Throw with force
6. "Hang ___ your hats"
7. Albino lab rodent
8. "Fiddler on the Roof" setting
9. "St. Elmo's Fire" singer John
10. "Diamonds ____ Girl's Best Friend"
11. "The Wizard of Oz" farm hand
19. "Do no harm" org.
20. 19th Greek letter
21. Ascending sizes, briefly
24. Cul-de-sacs
25. "Prince Valiant" character
26. Debilitate
30. Dreamed up
31. "Outer"
33. Arterial trunks
34. 3-D X-ray
35. "Quiet!"
36. "_____ Wednesday"
39. "Fortune" subjects
40. A semi lacks a front one
41. Aggravate
42. _____ gras
43. "Ah so!"
47. Big fuss

Answers on page 245.

WOMENS' FIRSTS IN SPORTS

ACROSS

1. Computer expert, for short
5. Chitchat
9. "Leverage" network
12. Ending with hard or soft
13. Alda of "M*A*S*H"
14. Balloon filler
15. Assayers' stuff
16. ___ de gallo (Mexican salsa)
17. Aircraft compartment
18. First African American woman to win Wimbledon
21. Oozes
22. Bearcat maker
24. Bridge support
27. Others, to Ovid
28. First woman to win an Indy car race
33. Length x width
34. Like some muscles
35. Igneous rock source
37. Young ladies, in Spanish: abbr.
41. First woman to win medals in three Olympic events
45. Small role
46. Amble
47. "___ From Muskogee"
48. "Rocks"
49. "Why would ___?"
50. Blow off steam
51. His day is celebrated in June
52. "___ of Eden"
53. Tolkien creatures

DOWN

1. MTV reality show, with "Days"
2. Noblemen
3. Greek Island
4. Politically correct pronoun
5. Where to taste tostone
6. Alter ego of Borat and Brüno
7. Scott Peterson's late wife
8. Controls
9. Middle Eastern salad
10. Connecticut town near New London
11. "Don't give up!"
19. "Beowulf," e.g.
20. Antares, for one
23. "Ghost Adventures" Lost Bagans
25. G.I.'s address
26. List of prior arrests
28. Beaver's work
29. Coffee bean variety
30. Nullified
31. Foot
32. Banks from the runway
36. Cliffside dwelling
38. Stash of riches
39. "American Idol" success Clay
40. Peter, Paul or Mary
42. "J'accuse" author Emile
43. "We try harder" company
44. Adjusts, as a clock
45. eBay offer

Answers on page 245.

AIM HIGHER

ACROSS

1. Prepare to swallow
5. High points: abbr.
8. Arnold of "True Lies"
11. Sleek, for short
12. Back-to-work joy: abbr.
13. Brain area
14. Cuban dance
16. Prayer ending
17. Noted plus-size model
18. Yogurt franchise
19. St. Paul's neighbor, for short
22. "Return of the Jedi" creature
24. Fresh start
25. Barely make it
29. Its capital hosted the 2002 Olympics
30. Dingo home: abbr.
31. N.Y.C. cultural center: abbr.
32. Provided that
34. Reprimand, with "out"
35. Close, as an envelope
36. Dentist's direction
37. "Holy mackerel!"
39. "Come again?"
41. Gold for a miner
42. Brazilian martial art: hyph.
46. Collapsed
47. 66, e.g.: abbr.
48. "My bad!"
49. Genetic building block
50. Diffident
51. Wyle of "ER"

DOWN

1. Alley animal
2. Laugh sound
3. Shakespeare's before
4. Start of a quote by Timothy Leary
5. "Tasty!"
6. Quote, part 2
7. _____-Caps
8. _____ of the Unknowns
9. Comply with
10. Quote, part 3
13. End of the quote
15. "Julie & Julia" actress Adams
18. Piggy digit
19. 1986 Art Spiegelman book
20. "What's gotten _____ you?"
21. Patricia of "Hud"
23. Milquetoast
25. "Roots," e.g.
26. Zen riddle
27. Z-series and F-series, for example
28. Its motto is "*Lux et veritas*"
33. _____ Perce tribe
36. British rule in colonial India
37. _____ of Arc
38. "Giant" author Ferber
40. "Hip to Be Square" rocker Lewis
41. Drug associated with Timothy Leary
42. 11th graders: abbr.
43. "_____ bad!"
44. Marienbad, for one
45. Show to a seat, slangily

Answers on page 245.

KITCHEN CONFIDENT

ACROSS

1. Common measure in the kitchen: abbr.
4. Movie-rating org.: abbr.
8. Farm mother
11. Soybean paste
13. Take home
14. "Hold On Tight" rock group
15. Kitchen personality born 2/2/1948 in Brooklyn
17. Franken and Gore
18. Kitchen personality born 8/25/1968 in Glens Falls
20. Reacts to yeast
23. Tater _____
24. Scrap of food
25. Arcane
30. Kitchen personality born 8/3/1941 in Jersey City
33. "Likely story"
34. Pin number?
35. It comes twice after "oom"
36. Nourishes
38. Kitchen personality born 8/15/1912 in Pasadena
43. Pay dirt
44. Kitchen personality born 1/19/1947 in Albany
48. Saltshaker letter, sometimes
49. Commits a faux pas
50. Himalayan legend
51. Part of U.N.L.V.
52. Facts and figures
53. Lenient

DOWN

1. "More than I needed to know!": abbr.
2. Biblical no-no
3. Free TV ad: abbr.
4. Classic Ford vehicle, for short
5. Trail
6. Realm
7. One of the original Mouseketeers
8. Certain vital sign
9. Jazzy Fitzgerald
10. Prying
12. Nightmarish boss
16. Small batteries
19. MGM founder whose name is on many movie theaters
20. "_____ and Michele's High School Reunion"
21. "Dies _____" (hymn)
22. Like some prom dresses
25. Melted glace
26. Ukraine or Lithuania, once: abbr.
27. Suffix with Capri
28. Ticked off
29. Egg holders: abbr.
31. Cuisine choice that sounds like a piece of neckwear
32. Like some football goalposts
36. Neighbor of Ala. and Ga.
37. Small whirlpool
38. Piano man Billy
39. _____ Major (constellation)

40. Irene of "Fame"
41. Injured
42. Ingrid's role in "Casablanca"
45. Slim swimmer

46. J.F.K. info
47. Put the kibosh on

1	2	3			4	5	6	7		8	9	10
11			12		13					14		
15				16						17		
			18						19			
20	21	22						23				
24				25	26	27					28	29
30			31	32								
33									34			
		35					36	37				
38	39				40	41	42					
43				44							45	46	47
48				49					50			
51				52						53		

125

CUT CORNERS

ACROSS

1. Budgeting pro, abbr.
4. All over again
8. "Can't Help Lovin' _____ Man" ("Shaw Band" song)
11. Curve
12. "Me neither!"
13. "And," in Swedish
14. Utah's nickname
17. Giant, in folklore
18. Abduct
20. 1996 loser to Bill Clinton
24. Stable outburst
25. Adidas alternative
27. Beat easily
28. Alien art form, some say
32. "Mercury" indie rock band _____ Party
33. Engrave
34. Combines
36. Carpet for the '70s
41. Return announcement
43. 2001 Ethan Hawke film
44. Expectant baby, colloquially
48. "... _____ quit!"
49. Banish
50. "The Lord of the Rings" creature
51. Jay-Z city
52. "Hercules" TV spin-off
53. "Angels of mercy," briefly

DOWN

1. Dish on a stick: var.
2. "Grazie" response in a Dean Martin song
3. Acidic
4. "32 Flavors" singer DiFranco
5. Thanksgiving month: abbr.
6. Shortly before?
7. "Ring around the collar" brand
8. Negotiate with success
9. Kindergarten admonition
10. All of history
15. "If only _____ listened!"
16. "Cat on a Hot _____ Roof"
19. A Dr. has one
21. "Night," to "day": abbr.
22. "Fortune" founder Henry
23. Discharges
26. Aqueduct feature
28. Board
29. Will Ferrell's "A Night at the _____ "
30. "Lost" airline
31. Said twice, a Latin dance
32. ASCAP alternative
35. "Mythbusters" subj.
37. '60s Pontiac muscle car
38. All-night partyer
39. An Ivy, briefly
40. Chaps, for short
42. "Goldfinger" fort
45. Before Wed.
46. 24-hr. buying channel
47. "H" as in Herakles

1	2	3		4	5	6	7		8	9	10
11				12					13		
14			15					16			
17							18				
20				21	22	23		24			
				25			26		27		
	28	29	30					31			
32					33						
34				35		36			37	38	39
41					42				43		
	44					45	46	47			
	48				49					50	
	51				52					53	

Answers on page 246.

OUTFITTED FOR SUCCESS

ACROSS

1. Piece of lamb
5. Nudge
8. Catch, as flies
12. The "A" in A.D.
13. Bar code: abbr.
14. Famed liner, briefly
15. Waves
16. Art director on "Mad Men"
17. Cemetery sights
18. Have an appearance that is suitable for a job
21. Washington, e.g.: abbr.
22. In favor of
23. Clairvoyance, e.g.
26. Cashew, e.g.
28. Dog restraint
32. Be evasive
35. "The universal donor" of blood
36. Like wheat
37. Census datum
38. "My New _____" (Paris Hilton reality show)
40. Oolong, for one
42. "Graveyard" employees
48. Catcall
49. Loo, for short
50. Brawl
51. "L'_____, c'est moi"
52. Female sheep
53. About
54. Plus
55. Ring bearer, maybe
56. _____ tide

DOWN

1. "Beverly Hills Cop" org.
2. Remarkable person
3. About, on a memo
4. Asian menu promise
5. New
6. Brightly colored fish
7. Staff leader?
8. Nerds
9. Frau's partner
10. "_____ it the truth!"
11. Soldiers
19. Dispatched
20. More civil
23. NYC time
24. _____ blue, in hopscotch
25. Member of Gladys Knight's group
27. Even if, briefly
29. Hoofed animal
30. "So _____ me!"
31. "Jonah _____"
33. Comeback
34. Dine at a chum's
39. Army base near Petersburg, Va.
41. Canton neighbor
42. Alien org.
43. Furnace output
44. Trumpet sound
45. Cork's country
46. Santa _____, California
47. "Cut it out!"
48. Feast of Lights observer

Answers on page 246.

SOME THINGS FOR A WEDDING DRESS

ACROSS

1. Bewildered utterances
5. Ponzi scheme, e.g.
9. Marvelous, in slang
12. Cup part
13. Halo, e.g.
14. "Do Ya" rock grp.
15. 1957 Disney classic
17. _____ juice (milk)
18. They bought out Cingular
19. Jeer
21. Early presidential primary state
26. "Are you a man, _____ mouse?"
27. Brand-name pot scrubber
28. Burger topping: abbr.
30. Even if, briefly
31. "A Day Without Rain" artist
35. Understanding
38. If wild, sow it
39. A daredevil may be living on this
42. "In what way?"
43. The tax man
44. East ender?
45. Wireless networking protocol
51. Charlotte-to-Raleigh dir.
52. "_____ of Eden"
53. Epps of "House"
54. Certain digital watch face, for short
55. Colors
56. Tent supporters

DOWN

1. "True Blood" network
2. Web domain: abbr.
3. Cached
4. Rock singer Patty
5. HAL's 2010 equivalent
6. _____-de-sac
7. "_____ we having fun yet?"
8. Cooking personality Stewart
9. Leg part
10. "Home _____"
11. Toss out
16. Flight data, briefly
20. Capitol Hill worker
21. _____ de plume
22. Renaissance, for one
23. "All for one and one for all," e.g.
24. "Don't give me that!"
25. Center to edge connector, on a bike
29. "One of _____" (Willa Cather novel)
32. Noxious
33. Starchy tuber
34. Absorbed, as a cost
36. Investigated
37. Cut, maybe
39. Carried
40. Confessed, with "up"
41. Band
42. Command to a dog
46. Put down
47. "It's no _____!"
48. Aliens, for short

49. Mark
50. Mins. and mins.

ACROSS

1. Biceps-building exercise
5. Hosp. area
8. FBI guys
12. Length times width, for a rectangle
13. "Smoking or _____?"
14. All-night party
15. French bread
17. Touched Down
18. Imp
20. "Am I a god _____ dog?" (Kipling)
21. Cold War president, familiarly
22. Locks on a lion
24. Spread similar to rillettes
26. Nameless one
29. Fergie's group
32. Have a bug
33. Recognized, briefly
34. Donations
35. Medical suffix
36. Word before "that" or "there"
37. Military procession
42. Heckle
43. Pooped
45. Prefix with "potent" or "present"
46. A cat may look _____ king
47. Memo opening
48. Travel bag
49. Room with microscopes
50. Gas used in signs

DOWN

1. Truck section
2. River through Kazakhstan
3. Like some tournaments
4. Toulouse-_____
5. Like Olympic competitions: abbr.
6. _____ d'Azur
7. Like a rough draft
8. Serious
9. French Sudan, today
10. Immoral
11. Circus sight
16. Fraternity vowel
19. _____ out (just got by)
22. Industrialist's deg.
23. Actress Larter
24. Supporter, often
25. Positive vote
26. "Great work!"
27. Overact
28. CIA predecessor
30. Snow White waker
31. Cause defender
35. Otherworldly
36. "What _____ you getting at?"
37. Kind of tape
38. Show that premiered on Broadway in 1996
39. Falafel wrap
40. Appaloosa alternative
41. Two-tone coin
42. Scribble (down)
44. Perfect beauty, slangily

Answers on page 246.

LOOKING FOR MR. BIG

ACROSS

1. Genesis grandchild
5. Not clerical
9. Yukon maker
12. "A Mighty Wind" actor Eugene
13. Coin that debuted on 1/1/02
14. Crowd cry
15. Petit four finisher
16. Smell
17. Fire
18. Star of 28-ACROSS
21. Paul Anka's birthplace
22. Word after Nine or Kanye
23. Sportage maker
24. Singer Franklin
28. TV series made into a 2008 movie
33. Invisible
34. Born, in Bordeaux
35. Stapleton of "All in the Family"
38. Speaks pompously
40. Star of 28-ACROSS
44. Purge
45. Prefix with potent
46. Hawaiian feast
48. Brian of ambient music
49. "How awful!"
50. ER tests
51. Chicago superstation
52. Lisa Simpson, for one
53. _____ butter

DOWN

1. Carmaker Ransom _____ Olds
2. Part of Annie Hall's attire
3. Go heavy on the levy
4. Lake Assad setting
5. Skintight wear
6. A8 maker
7. Remove creases from
8. Bundle binder
9. It may be unmarked
10. Long skirts
11. Word after hope or treasure
19. 2001 NFL Hall of Fame inductee Lynn
20. "Never Wave at _____" (1952 film)
21. Go-aheads
25. It ends in septembre
26. Satirical weekly newspaper
27. ___ Bendel (Fifth Avenue boutique)
29. Family reunion attendee
30. Communicating
31. "_____ Mutant Ninja Turtles"
32. "_____ we can!" (Obama mantra)
35. Where Michelle Obama shops
36. Watching
37. Off _____ (occasionally)
39. Semi bars
41. Catcall
42. Chat room initialism
43. Year, on monuments
47. "_____ Today"

Answers on page 246.

WOODY ALLEN FILMS

ACROSS

1. Turturro of "The Sopranos"
5. Having the skill
9. "The Sopranos" group
12. Greeting to the chief
13. Slinky's shape
14. Pal of Tarzan
15. 1977 Woody Allen movie
17. Long of "Soul Food"
18. Tool for Paul Bunyan
19. Old-time anesthetic
21. "Who's on _____?"
24. Justice Sotomayor
26. "_____ Today" (newspaper)
27. Caboose's place
29. Sicilian spewer
32. Took charge
33. 1990 Woody Allen movie
35. Hamilton's bill
36. Explorer Ericson
38. Verbally assault
39. _____ deco
40. Double reeds
42. Breaker of Aaron's homer record
44. "Barbarella" director Roger
46. Voice man Blanc
47. Rebel org. in "Michael Collins"
48. 1978 Woody Allen movie
54. Tofu source
55. Work hard
56. Perfume holder
57. Much computer spam
58. "Now!" in the ER
59. Ticklish one on "Sesame Street"

DOWN

1. "Gotcha!"
2. James Bond creator Fleming
3. Loud disturbance
4. Name after "AKA"
5. Need aspirin
6. Feathery wrap
7. Rap's _____ Kim
8. Former "American Idol" judge
9. 1979 Woody Allen movie
10. Andy Taylor's boy
11. Yogi or Boo-Boo
16. Newsboy's cry, once
20. Cause for overtime
21. Having no vacancies
22. Crystal ball–reader's words
23. 1987 Woody Allen movie
24. Takes a cruise
25. Killer whale
28. "What _____ is new?"
30. Social goofball
31. Pantry pests
34. Sign of a dying fire
37. Scully's org. on "The X-Files"
41. Leaves off
43. Martini garnish
44. American Express rival
45. Yankee slugger, for short
46. Cheesy sandwich
49. The "N" in NIMBY
50. _____ Maria (liqueur)
51. Olive or grapeseed
52. Battering tool
53. _____-pitch softball

Answers on page 247.

...BUT I PLAY ONE ON TV

ACROSS

1. Easy mark
4. Rework, in a way
8. Sitter's bane
12. Time period
13. Poor, as excuses go
14. Actor's part
15. Dr. _____ (Bill Cosby role)
18. Muscular fitness
19. Poker champ _____ Ungar
20. Dawn until dusk
23. Eggs companion
28. _____-mo
31. Sci-fi escape vehicles
34. Show concern
35. Dr. _____ (Alan Alda role)
38. Neck of the woods
39. Epps or Sharif
40. Hippie's place to "crash"
41. Powerful ray
43. Neptune's realm
45. Chocolate dog, for short
48. Use a cattle prod on
52. Dr. _____ (Lorraine Bracco role)
58. Opera highlight
59. Burn treatment
60. Slip up
61. Disappear, like the Wicked Witch
62. Foam at the mouth
63. "_____ milk?"

DOWN

1. Religious splinter group
2. Woody's folksy son
3. Annoying kid
4. Keebler pitchman
5. Morse unit
6. Radio personality Don _____
7. Contact via cell phone, in a way
8. Lingerie buy
9. One of the Lowes
10. Every last bit
11. _____ time (course slot)
16. G-man
17. Butter holder
21. Big galoot
22. "Walk the dog" toy
24. Unreturnable serve
25. Fish in gefilte fish
26. Willy in "Free Willy"
27. Scholarship criterion
28. Counterfeit
29. "Tomb raider" Croft
30. Wilson of "Wedding Crashers"
32. Pelosi's party: abbr.
33. Hydrotherapy locales
36. Kit _____ (candy brand)
37. Intense wrath
42. _____ G (Baron Cohen character)
44. Stat often lied about
46. Way out there
47. Lugosi of horror films
49. Designer Cassini

50. Hairdo for Michael Jackson
51. Gossips dish it
52. Printer or copier problem
53. Bard's before
54. Zilch

55. Father on "Curb Your Enthusiasm"
56. Harry Potter pal _____ Weasley
57. Subway Series player

Answers on page 247.

ACROSS

1. "Weeds" network, for short
4. Humpty Dumpty took one
8. Gorilla or chimp
11. "Flags of _____ Fathers"
12. Natural healing plant
13. Got grayer
14. 2008 Miley Cyrus album
16. "Auld _____ Syne"
17. "Quiet on the _____!"
18. Ralph Kramden's sitcom wife
19. German autos with four-ring logos
22. Web video gear, for short
24. Homer Simpson neighbor _____ Flanders
25. On the bounding main
26. Shoreline indentations
28. Character played by Miley Cyrus
33. Martin _____ of "The West Wing"
34. Simon Cowell's show, for short
35. Dry, on a wine bottle
38. Gallery display
39. Beat the goalie, say
40. Fanzine subject, for short
42. Comics squeal
43. Dry, like the Sahara
44. Miley Cyrus's country-singer dad
49. Lens holders
50. Like dental surgery
51. The Grand _____ Opry
52. Presidents' Day mo.
53. Folks to hang with
54. Take the gold

DOWN

1. Have a good cry
2. Movie charioteer Ben-_____
3. Stuff to smelt
4. Pretends to have, as an injury
5. Oodles
6. Mary's boss on "The Mary Tyler Moore Show"
7. "Live and _____ Die"
8. "See You _____" (2007 Miley Cyrus single)
9. Brit's coins
10. Defeated, but barely
13. The whole enchilada
15. Chinese, Indians, Pakistanis, etc.
18. Congregation response
19. Sound from a massage table
20. Springsteen's birthplace of song
21. Comfy room
22. Halley's _____
23. Bell-ringing cosmetics company
26. Oscar winner for "Moonstruck"
27. Like a Post-it note
29. Moby Dick's pursuer
30. "Without further..."
31. "Neither snow _____ rain..."
32. Hoppy brew

35. Neck warmer
36. Like "The Twilight Zone" episodes
37. "The _____" (2009 Miley Cyrus single)
39. Unloads on eBay
41. Newspaper execs: abbr.

42. Airline to Israel
44. Dizzy Gillespie's jazz genre
45. Investment that may be rolled over, for short
46. Man the oars
47. MacGraw of "Love Story"
48. Cash in Japan

1	2	3		4	5	6	7		8	9	10
11				12				13			
14			15					16			
			17				18				
19	20	21				22	23		24		
25					26			27			
28			29					30	31	32	
		33					34				
35	36	37		38			39				
40			41			42					
43				44	45			46	47	48	
49				50				51			
52				53				54			

Answers on page 247.

DESPERATE HOUSEWIVES

ACROSS

1. "There once ..." (limerick start)
4. Compass lines
8. Use a pogo stick
11. Play part
12. Sans accompaniment
13. Two-thumbs-up review
14. Edie Britt portrayer Nicol-lette _____
16. Perched on
17. Hefty sandwich
18. Wild-eyed and crazy
20. Part of a drum kit
23. Went in a hurry
26. Start a Texas hold'em hand
28. Superman portrayer Christo-pher _____
29. Scrooge's outburst
32. Bree Van de Kamp player Marcia _____
34. Southern soldier, for short
35. Mistreat physically
37. Risked a ticket, maybe
39. Stick up for
41. Highly capable
44. Big bashes
46. J.Lo's husband, _____ Anthony
48. Way on or off an expressway
50. Gabrielle Solis player Eva _____ Parker
53. Chapters of history
54. Creative flash
55. The "I" of TGIF
56. Bear's lair
57. Lumberyard tools
58. Get firm

DOWN

1. Help with the dishes
2. Feels sore
3. Shock jock Howard
4. "Just _____ suspected!"
5. Curtain holder
6. Chowder morsel
7. Fish-finding device
8. Susan Mayer portrayer Teri _____
9. Lacto-_____-vegetarian
10. Get-up-and-go
13. Reward for excellent work
15. On the _____ (traveling)
19. Sipped slowly
21. Not long past
22. Something to lend or bend
24. Exile from Eden
25. Society newbie, for short
27. Rock's _____ Lobos
29. No longer edible
30. _____ Vigoda of "Fish"
31. Lynette Scavo player Felic-ity _____
33. Place for rest cure
36. Flows through the cracks
38. Floor model
40. Places to buy cold cuts
42. Left Bank city
43. Like many a cliché
45. Scotch's mixer
47. Playbill listing

48. Visibly embarrassed
49. "You _____" (Lionel Richie hit)
51. Still in the package
52. Fuel for some artificial logs

Answers on page 247.

THE SIMPSON FAMILY

ACROSS

1. Artist's topper
6. Belt overhang
9. See 27-DOWN
12. Quick on one's feet
13. Blond shade
14. Sheep's utterance
15. The Duff beer-drinking Simpson
16. "_____ whiz!"
17. Make a boo-boo
18. _____ and vigor
20. "The Simpsons" creator _____ Groening
22. Toss in a chip
25. Catchall category
28. Like excellent corned beef
29. Tennis club figure
30. T-shirt or blouse, e.g.
33. "The Simpsons" network
34. Golf or bowling target
35. Outburst from 15-ACROSS
37. Vardalos of "My Big Fat Greek Wedding"
39. _____ out (barely manage)
40. Carpet feature
41. Cab-door postings
43. Lecher's look
44. "_____in Hell" (comic strip in which 10-Down first appeared)
46. Possible tic-tac-toe outcome
48. _____ bulb (not-too-bright sort)
49. "Cheers" bartender
52. The blue-haired Simpson
56. "Burn Notice" network
57. Cheer to a toreador
58. "The _____" (everyday bar order)
59. Rock's Steely _____
60. Movies, for short
61. Oozes slowly

DOWN

1. "_____ humbug!"
2. Swellhead's problem
3. Place for a basketball net
4. Time for the late news
5. _____ Polo of "Meet the Fockers"
6. Prankster's bit
7. "_____ as directed"
8. "The Simpsons," for this puzzle
9. Aid illegally
10. The mischievous Simpson
11. Musical gift
19. Young tyke
21. Busts, oils, etc.
22. Cuddly TV extraterrestrial
23. Sign gas
24. Sitcom set at the Sunshine Cab Company
26. Three-wheeler
27. With 9-ACROSS, nickname for our 16th president
31. Garfield's canine pal
32. Vaulter's need
36. "Hannah and _____ Sisters"
38. Comics bark

40. Child's "magic word"
42. Fables writer of old
44. The precocious Simpson
45. David Bowie's model wife
47. Shock jock Don _____
48. Broadway flop

50. Boxer portrayed by Will Smith
51. Tex-_____ cuisine
53. Feel remorse over
54. Big name in clothing retail
55. Chicago rails, for short

1	2	3	4	5		6	7	8		9	10	11
12						13				14		
15						16				17		
		18		19			20	21			
22	23	24			25	26	27					
28					29					30	31	32
33					34					35		36
	37		38		39				40			
		41	42						43			
	44	45					46	47				
48				49	50	51		52		53	54	55
56				57				58			
59				60				61			

Answers on page 247.

ROCK & ROLL HALL OF FAMERS

ACROSS

1. Stinging remark
5. "What's up, _____?"
8. Indulge in self-praise
12. Inventor's germ
13. Savings option, briefly
14. "The Tonight Show" host
15. "Still The Same" singer, and 2004 Rock and Roll Hall of Fame inductee
17. "I'm _____ your tricks!"
18. Onassis, in headlines
19. Touched down on the runway
21. Break up
23. "There's more . . ."
24. Prankster's ammo
25. Train component
27. Beauty queen's topper
31. Keeping one's cool
33. Had an edge
35. Airline to Israel
36. Mascara mess
38. Club _____ (resort)
40. _____ for (choose)
41. _____ and don'ts
43. Goes on a hunger strike
45. Disco light
48. Mentalist's skill, for short
49. Explorer Ponce de _____
50. "Jump" band, and 2007 Rock and Roll Hall of Fame inductees
55. Mineral abundant in spinach
56. Overhead railways, for short
57. Ruffle the feathers of
58. Pocket bread
59. Born, in society columns
60. Revise on a word processor

DOWN

1. Baby's splatter protector
2. Commotion
3. Confederate soldier, for short
4. _____ metabolism
5. Like clocks without hands
6. Unrefined metal
7. Rhea's "Cheers" role
8. "Heart of Glass" band, and 2006 Rock and Roll Hall of Fame inductees
9. Tear to bits
10. Start the pot
11. Well-mannered
16. Rocker Clapton
20. Bug in a hobby farm
21. Stitch line
22. Sickly looking
24. Alternatives to Macs
26. "Losing My Religion" band, and 2007 Rock and Roll Hall of Fame inductees
28. "Thanks _____!"
29. Performs like Eminem
30. Supermodel Carol _____
32. "Like a Virgin" singer, and 2008 Rock and Roll Hall of Fame inductee
34. One side in a football game
37. Stick up

39. 100-meter race, say
42. Dwarfs count
44. Bowler's pickup
45. Freudian _____
46. Actress Hatcher or Polo

47. Carrot or radish, e.g.
51. Brewpub offering
52. Coffee-to-go topper
53. Gridder _____ Manning
54. After-tax amount

1	2	3	4		5	6	7		8	9	10	11
12					13				14			
15				16					17			
			18				19	20				
	21	22					23					
24				25		26		27		28	29	30
31			32		33		34		35			
36				37		38		39		40		
			41		42		43		44			
45	46	47					48					
49					50	51				52	53	54
55					56				57			
58					59				60			

Answers on page 247.

LIZ'S LOVES

ACROSS
1. Keg outlet
4. Scratch up
7. Cheated, slangily
9. _____ and error
11. Liz Taylor husband #4, Eddie _____
12. Liz Taylor husband #1, Nicky _____
14. Tax-collecting org.
15. Reacts to yeast
17. Tot's "piggy"
18. Born, in bridal bios
19. Designer Diane _____ Furstenberg
20. Take a break
21. Mag staffers: abbr.
22. Hair goo
23. Hospital helpers
24. Liz Taylor husband #2, Michael _____
26. Bargain events
29. Travel stopover
30. __ up (absorb)
33. Got a great grade on
34. "The Producers" director _____ Brooks
35. Prefix with cycle or angle
36. Chowed down
37. Clear kitchen wrap
39. Poem of praise
40. Liz Taylor husband #5, Richard _____
42. Liz Taylor husband #6, John _____

44. Long-lasting curls
45. Villainous look
46. Pre-Easter buy
47. Words from sponsors

DOWN
1. Prepares, as a salad
2. Barbecue residue
3. Look through a telescope
4. Diagnostic scans: abbr.
5. Have a bug
6. Turned informer
7. Added to the payroll
8. Utter nonsense
9. "In that case . . ."
10. Ready to fall out
11. Parking violation penalty
13. Butterfly catchers' gear
16. Military man
20. Fix, as a fight
22. U.S. military men
23. Raggedy doll
24. Get hitched
25. The Bunkers, to Mike Stivic
26. Swedish auto
27. Behave badly
28. Looked lustfully
30. Mick Jagger's group, for short
31. "Law & _____"
32. Place to dock
34. Le _____ (auto race)
37. Just a few
38. Granny
41. Take a taste of
43. Checkers color

Answers on page 248.

AT THE MOVIES

ACROSS

1. Subject of an APB
5. Hematite and cinnabar
9. Nourished
12. Finished
13. Nonkosher meat
14. Thurman of "Kill Bill" films
15. Ali MacGraw chick flick of 1970
17. Tiny insect
18. Clenched hand
19. December visitor
21. "What _____ Want" (2000 chick flick)
24. Actor Sinise
25. Opened just a tad
26. Egg-white concoction
30. Ronald Reagan was once its president: abbr.
31. With 23-DOWN, Sally Field chick flick of 1980
32. April 15 addressee
33. Small change
35. Bureau attachment
36. Responsibility
37. Veil material
38. "_____ Me" (1984 Steve Martin film)
40. It may be balanced
42. Half of CIV
43. Kevin Bacon chick flick of 1984
48. Where to get into hot water?
49. Old Roman coins
50. Custard dessert
51. CIA predecessor
52. Airline to Jerusalem
53. Extravagant party

DOWN

1. D.C. VIP
2. Bolivian president Morales
3. Start, as an engine
4. "Gentlemen _____ Blondes" (1953 Marilyn Monroe)
5. Withdraws, with "out"
6. Underground transport?
7. Get it wrong
8. Uppermost ship propeller
9. Barbra Streisand chick flick of 1968
10. Give off
11. Statistician's info
16. Transgression
20. Son of Prince Valiant
21. Vespiary resident
22. City northeast of L.A.
23. See 31-ACROSS
24. Jennifer in "Dirty Dancing"
26. Atlas abbr.
27. Wide shoe spec
28. Russian river
29. Italy's villa d'_____
31. Fluffy dessert
34. LP filler
35. Isolated (from)
37. Business card: abbr.
38. Furthermore
39. They may be glossed over
40. Explorer on Nick Jr.

41. Leaning letters: abbr.
44. Fry scallops in this
45. "Bravo" at a bullfight
46. Precollege exam
47. Raleigh-to-Norfolk dir.

 Answers on page 248.

BAR TRENDS

ACROSS

1. Oscar Night sight
5. Enormous
9. Gift decoration
12. Last word of "Good Bless America"
13. Writer Wiesel
14. Pumpernickel alternative
15. From the start
16. Just short of 10 times as much
18. Classic cocktail garnished with lime
20. Riddle-me-_____
21. Spreadsheet program
24. Cocktail with amaretto and vodka
29. Argentite, e.g.
30. Tori of pop music
31. Perfect score in diving
32. Trash bag brand
33. Ayres who played Dr. Kildare
34. Cocktail with tequila and orange-flavored liqueur
36. Lennox of the Eurythmics
38. Color TV pioneer
39. Cocktail with vermouth and fruit
45. Trafalgar Square statue honoree
47. Get _____ the act
48. Kwik-E-Mart clerk on "The Simpsons"
49. Feminine suffix
50. Worry
51. Long-nosed fish
52. Leonine outburst
53. Scream

DOWN

1. Thick carpeting
2. Literature Nobelist Morrison
3. "You said it!"
4. Microwaves anew
5. Prolonged feud
6. Came down to earth
7. Chinese: prefixes
8. Target MTV audience member
9. Variety of cabbage
10. Popeye's Olive _____
11. Joined in matrimony
17. Mend
19. Conservative leader?
22. Part of QED
23. Helen of Troy's mother
24. Festive event
25. Harbinger
26. Heavy rainfall
27. Part of HMS
28. Certain impressionist
32. Delight
34. Insufficient
35. Direction that this clue is not: abbr.
37. Comparatively more: suffix
40. Nevada Museum of Art site
41. Winona's "Dracula" role
42. Pertaining to
43. Present time
44. Part of IHOP

45. Prank

46. Pollution control gp.

MRS. PRESIDENT

ACROSS

1. _____ standstill
4. Noise made by ewe?
7. South American country with president Michelle Bachelet
12. Total
13. Maze goal
14. Integrity
15. European country with president Mary McAleese
17. Billionaire corporate raider Carl
18. Get scratchy
19. Animal life in certain areas
20. Thoroughbred's walks
21. Give approval
22. Fairy tale starter
23. Lisa Simpson's brother
24. South American country with president Cristina Fernandez de Kirchner
28. Court figure: abbr.
29. Acronym that sometimes means "right now"
32. R&B singer with the 2008 album "The Declaration"
36. Skip class
37. Amount on a credit card statement
38. Eat extremely fast
39. Poi-making roots
40. African country with president Ellen Johnson-Sirleaf
41. "_____ to the doctor..."
42. "Un momento, _____ favor"
43. "_____ not fair!"
44. Asian country with president Pratibha Patil
45. Mrs., in Madrid
46. Nay's opposite

DOWN

1. Grated Italian cheese
2. Wrapped headdress
3. First name on the "Ugly Betty" set
4. Necklace pieces
5. Name for two wives of Henry VIII
6. Put 2 and 2 together?
7. Dry Italian red wine
8. "_____ pocus!"
9. Insipid
10. Razzie Award-winning actress Lindsay
11. Young's partner in accounting
16. "See ya!"
19. Eight quintupled
21. "Birds fly over the rainbow. Why then, oh why _____?"
23. Joan's "Whatever Happened to Baby Jane?" costar
25. Hardcore rap genre
26. Not so worldly-wise
27. New York's Waldorf-_____ Hotel
30. Keenness of perception, especially with vision
31. "Wheel of Fortune" category

32. The middle of a play
33. Olympic gymnast Johnson
34. Moved quickly, like some hunting predators
35. Rice-_____ ("The San Francisco Treat")

36. "Will & Grace" star Messing
38. Fashion legend Christian
40. CD predecessors: abbr.

Answers on page 248.

FOOD FOR SKIN CARE

ACROSS

1. Parsley serving
6. They take W-2s: abbr.
9. Hosp. scanner: abbr.
12. Spotted laugher
13. Chess pieces, collectively (even the queen)
14. Unleaded counterpart: abbr.
15. Actor Baldwin and novelist Waugh, for two
16. Fruit high in omega-3 fatty acids, to keep skin plump
18. Italian frozen dessert
20. It gets rid of leg stubble
21. Adam of "The Wedding Singer"
24. Drink with some anti-inflammatory properties, and full of antioxidants
27. "Mamma Mia!" basis
31. "Atlas Shrugged" author Rand
32. Pottery class fixtures
34. Rock's _____ Speedwagon
35. Answering machine noise
37. Fish (like other oily fish) high in omega-3 fatty acids, keeping skin from drying out
39. Length of some basic warranties
41. Drink with marshmallows
44. Paper fastener
48. Vegetable with lots of beta-carotene, converted to vitamin A for skin health
51. Second-largest city on the Ruhr
52. Roswell craft: abbr.
53. Treasure hunt need
54. Do the totals again
55. Sony handheld gaming system, for short: abbr.
56. Like some winter weather
57. French : Mlles :: Spanish : _____

DOWN

1. Fuzzy carpet
2. TV's Gomer or actress Missi
3. Film projector need
4. As a precaution
5. It gets filled at a filling station
6. "_____ little teapot . . ."
7. Hit the gas pedal in neutral
8. Be a loud sleeper
9. "We Sing. We Dance. We Steal Things." singer Jason
10. Decorate again
11. Dr. Frankenstein's go-to guy
17. Actress Irene of "Fame"
19. Promptly
22. Airport holdup
23. Jouster's weapons
24. Have a chat
25. Bread for a reuben
26. Dir. opposite WSW
28. "It's too cold out!"
29. Queen or drone
30. Company that introduced AIM
33. They're out at Rockefeller Center during the winter

36. 60% or below, usually
38. Pencil attachment
40. "The International" star Watts
41. Common bra size
42. They're clumsy
43. Cut part of a picture

45. Preparatory H.S. test
46. _____ charmed life
47. Comes to a close
49. "Tic _____ Dough" (1980s game show)
50. James Bond, e.g.

1	2	3	4	5	■	6	7	8	■	9	10	11
12						13				14		
15						16			17			
18					19	■		20				
■	■	■	21			22	23			■	■	■
24	25	26						■	27	28	29	30
31			■	32				33	■	34		
35			36	■	37				38			
■	■	■	39	40						■	■	■
41	42	43			■	■	44			45	46	47
48					49	50	■	51				
52			■	53				■	54			
55			■	56				■	57			

157   Answers on page 248.

IN THE BAG

ACROSS

1. Physicist Nikola
6. Russian fighter plane
9. Underwire locale
12. Legally prevent
13. Canoe propeller
14. "You've got Mail" co.
15. Item often found in a hand-bag
17. Truncate
18. Putter alternative
19. Lectures
21. Seuss or Spock
24. Pond fish
25. Demeanor
27. Place for poultry
30. Actress Gasteyer
31. Pound and Cornell
33. "Here _____ again!"
34. Absorbs, with "up"
36. Acquired
38. Traverse
40. Spreads joy
41. Available, at a bar
43. Hospital procedures: abbr.
44. Synth-pop artist Toro y _____
45. Item often found in a hand-bag
50. Down Under's "football" showdown: abbr.
51. Savings acct. plus
52. Got hitched again
53. Tattoo
54. Speck
55. Brainstorms

DOWN

1. Mike Hammer, for one
2. Boston–Cape Cod dir.
3. Letters on a Cardinal cap
4. Nabokov nymphet
5. Endorse
6. Site of 1969 landing
7. McKellan of "X-Men"
8. Actress Garbo
9. Item often found in a handbag
10. Corner chessboard piece
11. "The Sound of Music" setting
16. Junction of earth and sky
20. Circumference part
21. Financial transaction alias: abbr.
22. Wine: prefix
23. Item often found in a handbag
24. Holes on the moon
26. Sphere
28. S-shaped molding
29. They're full of beans
32. F. Murray Abraham's Oscar-winning role
35. Health resort
37. "Sorry _____!" ("Well excuse me!")
39. Plan-eating insect
41. Prefix with bus and directional
42. Norse goddess of fate
43. Canine hybrid
46. Plastic _____ Band
47. Female sheep
48. Verbal vote
49. Radical 1960s org.

Answers on page 248.

INEDIBLE EDIBLES

ACROSS

1. Breakfast drinks, for short
4. Web page language: abbr.
8. Cram into the overhead
12. Beluga delicacy
13. Black-and-white sandwich
14. Pretentious
15. Pitch thrown at the head
17. Pro _____ (in proportion)
18. Weaver's apparatus
19. Car parker
20. Fit of pique
22. Graphic often seen in an annual report
25. Double-reed woodwinds
27. "Fuhgeddaboudit!"
28. Young hospital helpers
34. Seashell seller
35. Cell phone's precursor
36. Attendance check
41. Fruit that sounds unattractive
42. "Old MacDonald" refrain
43. Car bar
45. Yalies
46. Amateur broadcaster's hobby
50. Splinter group
51. "Super Trouper" band
52. Make a choice
53. Time periods
54. Prone to prying
55. San Francisco's _____ Hill

DOWN

1. Sun or moon, poetically
2. Coffee, slangily
3. Marine mammal
4. Vagrant
5. Charlie Chaplin persona
6. Brooks of "Blazing Saddles"
7. Chatroom chuckle
8. Politico Palin
9. Singing syllables
10. Marine mammal
11. One of the Earp brothers
16. Well-known
19. TV screening device: hyph.
20. Part of SSN
21. Org. of Wizards and Magic
23. Silicon Valley giant
24. Corn serving
26. Big name in food service products
29. Singing group _____ Na Na
30. Former "American Idol" judge Abdul
31. Prodded
32. Fam. member
33. Madras Mr.
36. Della of "Touched by an Angel"
37. Persian Gulf ship
38. Nikon competitor
39. Menus, essentially
40. Symbols of meekness
44. Inside view: hyph.
46. Solo of "Star Wars"
47. Blood-typing letters
48. NYSE debut
49. NYC gambling parlor

Answers on page 249.

GENDER STUDIES

ACROSS

1. Hammett canine
5. Subside
8. Source of milk for Pecorino cheese
12. Criticize harshly
13. Latin possessive
14. Place with layers?
15. Suffragist jailed for voting in 1872
18. Empty _____ (one with grown children)
19. Decent
20. Wall St. debuts
22. Hamelin exterminator
25. Self-importance
28. Suffers
30. African flower?
31. Feminist social critic and author of "Vamps and Tramps"
34. Peel
35. Post an item on eBay
36. Van Gogh's amputation
37. NY city on the Mohawk
39. Jimmy of Led Zeppelin
41. Crooner Jerry
43. Russian ballerina Karsavina
47. Co-founder of "Ms." magazine
50. Geekazoid
51. "The Hustler" prop
52. Add, as cargo
53. Rockies tribe
54. Part of HRH
55. Jolly ol' academy

DOWN

1. Org.
2. Pivot
3. USSR news agency
4. Prized violin
5. Throws into confusion
6. "Maude" portrayer
7. Shotgun sound
8. Imitative
9. Log stack
10. Ages
11. Le Carre character
16. Kathmandu's country
17. Zenith
21. Catch some Zs
23. "East of Eden" director Kazan
24. Hitchcock's "_____ Window"
25. Light brown
26. Pony pace
27. One who'll eat anything
29. Sprinkle around
32. Bouncers' checks
33. Aquarium accumulation
38. Ryan's "Love Story" costar
40. Novelist Zola
42. Per
44. Med. school course
45. Start from scratch
46. "I agree!"
47. African antelope
48. Permit
49. Buddy Holly's "Peggy ___"

Answers on page 249.

BLACK EYED PEAS

ACROSS

1. In addition
5. French vineyard
8. Give a grade
12. Discusses again
14. Barely managed, with "out"
15. Black Eyed Peas song from album "The E.N.D."
17. Part of DJIA
18. Slalom shape
19. Tall and thin
20. Fender mishap
22. Spell
23. Very eager
25. *Joie de vivre*
27. Popular song
30. Black Eyed Peas song from album "The E.N.D."
33. Long or short measure
34. Peddle
35. Border on
36. Wine list option
37. Worker's compensation
39. Hollywood type
42. Photo, briefly
43. "_____ Lobo" (1970 John Wayne film)
46. Black Eyed Peas song from the album "Behind the Front"
49. Net
50. They're given out gratis
51. "_____ Wide Shut"
52. Greenspan's group: for short
53. Acapulco abode

DOWN

1. Parched
2. Alternative to Mega Bloks
3. Confrontation
4. Feed bag bit
5. Subdued
6. Gridiron "zebras," briefly
7. Employ
8. Chill out
9. Similar
10. Race that's approximately 6 miles long
11. Provocative
13. British submachine gun
16. Actress Verdugo
21. Faberge item
22. Genetically predisposed
23. "A Bug's Life" bug
24. Gloppy stuff
26. Cariou of Broadway
27. Classical Latin name for Ireland
28. Promissory note
29. Cable channel with the slogan "We Know Drama"
31. "_____ Heartbeat" (Amy Grant hit)
32. License plate
36. Lassos
38. Cause for a massage
39. Apex
40. Aiken of "American Idol"
41. Appropriate
42. Contaminant-free
44. March 15

45. Greek peak
47. Switch position
48. Epitome of simplicity

Answers on page 249.

KING OF COOL

ACROSS

1. Light source
5. "_____ Williams: The Adventure Begins..."
9. English spelling of what's heard before "gee"
12. Twin of Jacob
13. Tennis star Lendl
14. Madge and Millie's mother in "Picnic"
15. Polite fellow
16. "Miami _____"
17. Tracker maker
18. Paul Newman's directorial debut
21. Chart-topper
22. Grand _____ Opry
23. Troop troupe: abbr.
26. Opposite of Rep.
28. 1958 Paul Newman movie, "The _____, Hot Summer"
32. Paul Newman's film acting debut, with "The"
36. The Beatles' "_____ Love Her"
37. "Good Will Hunting" director Van Sant
38. Filming location
39. Actor Hunter in "The Life and Times of Judge Roy Bean"
42. Home of "The Real World"
44. Movie for which Paul Newman won his first acting Oscar, with "The"

50. Kimono tie
51. Burn remedy
52. Impartial
54. Punched-in-the-gut sound
55. "High Country" author Nevada
56. Either of two Roman statesmen
57. James Bond film, "Live and _____ Die"
58. Retired Atl. crossers
59. Make an afghan

DOWN

1. Ask for a handout
2. Data processing participant
3. Actress Turner
4. Paul Newman role _____ Cassidy
5. WWII icon Rosie the _____
6. Sam Raimi's "The _____ Dead"
7. Shortcut on a PC
8. "Paper Moon" star Ryan
9. What I will always follow?
10. Run off
11. Paul Newman movie, "Nobody's _____ "
19. Stay out of sight
20. 1954's "Riot in _____ Block 11"
23. Made in the _____
24. Sloth, for one
25. Spencer Tracy movie, "The _____ Man and the Sea"
27. "Charlie's Angels: Full

Throttle" director
29. Crankcase fluid
30. Sgt., e.g.
31. "I'll _____ you, my pretty, and your little dog, too!"
33. Don Corleone in "The God-father"
34. Gas-guzzling vehicles
35. Concerning or regarding
40. Some show horses: abbr.
41. Pampas weapons

43. Pullover feature, often
44. Paul Newman movie, "_____ Hand Luke"
45. Bassoon relative
46. Elevator, to a Brit
47. Paul Newman movie, "_____ Apache the Bronx"
48. "The Blackboard Jungle" author Hunter
49. Sherpa sighting
53. Do _____ disturb

THE ORIGINAL

ACROSS

1. Palindromic title
5. McAn of shoes
9. Base enforcers, for short
12. Comeback for "Are not!"
13. What Sweeney Todd cut
14. PC display
15. Character played by Johnny Depp in 38-ACROSS
18. Northwest state
19. Chopped liver spread
20. Foment anew
21. 1977 Marlo Thomas-Charles Grodin movie
24. Budget items
25. Director of 38-ACROSS
29. Hidden
30. 1979 Caine-Ustinov film
31. 1956 Glenn Ford western
36. End of winter
37. Mexican state bordering Arizona
38. 2009 Johnny Depp film
42. George Harrison hit "All Those Years _____"
43. The O'Haras' plantation
44. French state
45. "Win a Date _____ Hamilton!"
46. Trade
47. Hurl

DOWN

1. "_____ League" (1989 baseball movie)
2. Dean Martin song subject
3. Fire remains
4. "Flash Gordon" planet
5. Some pizza crust
6. Jack Black comedy "Shallow _____"
7. 1992 drama "Lorenzo's _____"
8. Hosp. test
9. He played the Old Man in "A Christmas Story"
10. Sixth-grader, usually
11. Underlying reason
16. Wall Street index, with "the"
17. Musical trio Salt _____
21. "Of _____ Sing"
22. Contained
23. Will Smith movie "_____ Legend"
24. League of Women Voters founder
25. Crazy in Yiddish
26. Johnny Depp's role in "Sleepy Hollow"
27. Emulate a snail
28. Egg layer
29. Stay put
31. 1970 Peter Boyle movie drama
32. Not taken care of, as in one's needs
33. Composer of opera "Mefistofele"
34. Quarters
35. Shoe trees

37. Simple task
39. Gene Kelly musical "_____ Always Fair Weather"
40. Crow's call
41. Cause that NOW championed

Answers on page 249.

AMERICAN GANGSTER

ACROSS

1. Tide type
4. Pillow protector
8. Evil lion in "The Lion King"
12. Undershirt neck shape
13. He played Largo in "Thunderball"
14. Mexican fast food
15. Keebler spokesman
16. Latin learner's verb
17. 1956 British tutor in Siam
18. Real-life boxer played by Denzel Washington
21. Trade shows
23. Big success
24. "_____ your pardon?"
25. Litigated
27. Sault _____ Marie, Michigan
30. Denzel Washington played a quadriplegic detective in this film, with "The"
33. Former Pink Floyd guitarist Barrett
34. Airline to Ben Gurion Airport
35. Operatic air
36. O'Hare airport designation
37. Doctoral dread
38. Oscar-winning film for Denzel Washington
43. In stitches
44. Watched
45. Light portable bed
48. It's all downhill from here
49. Actress Russo
50. Denzel Washington film, "Much _____ About Nothing"
51. "The _____ the limit!"
52. Denzel Washington, for one
53. President pro _____

DOWN

1. The night before
2. Canto lead-in
3. Cozy up to
4. Picket provokers
5. Prefix meaning "half"
6. "The Pelican Brief" director Pakula
7. "Man on Fire" co-star Radha
8. Word at a maze entrance
9. "I _____ hear you!"
10. Adolescent's skin outbreak
11. Sound at the circus
19. Egg on
20. Right-hand man
21. Little lies
22. Sondheim's "_____ Like That"
25. Denzel Washington movie, "A _____ Story"
26. Ending for spat or form?
27. Alley prowler
28. Work up a sweat
29. Stretches of time
31. Geneva research ctr.
32. "Fame" star Irene
36. Pen sounds
37. More out there
38. Cookbook meas.
39. Smell

40. Distant
41. Putin decline
42. Rowlands of "A Woman Under the Influence"

46. Stately poem
47. "Philadelphia" co-star Hanks

1	2	3		4	5	6	7		8	9	10	11
12				13					14			
15				16					17			
		18	19					20				
21	22						23					
24					25	26				27	28	29
30				31				32				
33				34					35			
			36					37				
38	39	40				41	42					
43					44					45	46	47
48				49					50			
51				52					53			

Answers on page 249.

OUR FAIR LADY

ACROSS

1. Greek letter
4. Govt. flight regulator
7. Held an election for
12. Actor Holm in "Robin and Marian"
13. Modern address (letters)
14. Marveled aloud
15. Muscular actor on "The A-Team"
16. Hoops org.
17. Having bristles, as wheat
18. 1959 Audrey Hepburn drama
21. Dreyer's ice cream, east of the Rockies
22. "Who am _____ judge?"
23. Asian cuisine
25. "Hallelujah, _____ Bum!" (1933 Al Jolson film)
26. Kettle and Barker
29. 1967 Audrey Hepburn thriller
33. Hockey great Bobby
34. "Death Be _____ Proud"
35. Actress Rossum who played Audrey in "The Audrey Hepburn Story"
36. Free radio ad: abbr.
37. Jack of "Kiss Me Deadly"
39. 1953 Audrey Hepburn romance
44. The end of _____
45. Vigor
46. Pasture plaint

48. "Let _____!" ("Go ahead!")
49. Action-film weapon
50. "Message _____ Bottle" (Kevin Costner movie)
51. Nature's soil
52. Part of a place setting
53. Substitute abbr., perhaps

DOWN

1. "Above the _____" (1994 basketball movie)
2. "Chicago" heroine Roxie _____
3. Being broadcast
4. "_____ Face" (Audrey Hepburn film)
5. "Damien: Omen II" actor
6. Actor Arkin in 29-ACROSS
7. Area prone to flooding
8. "_____ Steal a Million" (Audrey Hepburn movie)
9. "Yikes!"
10. Crystal ball consultant
11. Christian Science founder Mary Baker _____
19. Prepare for publication
20. _____ Valley, California
23. "_____ for the Road" (Audrey Hepburn movie)
24. One of a pair of hardy followers?
25. Hairy "Addams Family" character
26. Movie musical based on ABBA songs
27. "The Man with the Golden

_____ "(Sinatra movie)
28. "Blue _____" (1994 Jessica Lange movie)
30. Opens certain fasteners
31. Shipbuilder of old
32. "Wanted: _____ or Alive"
36. "_____ - When It Sizzles" (Audrey Hepburn movie)
37. Audrey's role in "My Fair Lady"

38. Speed to heed
39. _____-thin, like Audrey Hepburn was
40. Not taken in by
41. "A _____ formality!"
42. Largest cell in the human body
43. Tug
47. Motel rater

1	2	3		4	5	6		7	8	9	10	11
12				13				14				
15				16				17				
	18		19			20						
		21					22					
23	24					25				26	27	28
29				30	31			32				
33				34				35				
		36				37	38					
39	40	41			42					43		
44					45				46		47	
48					49				50			
51					52				53			

173

IMPERSONATION STATION

ACROSS

1. The Smashing Pumpkins' debut album
5. "Three Stooges" action
9. Guevara of Cuba
12. Kevin Kline's role in "A Fish Called Wanda"
13. Money drawer
14. '50s school dance
15. "_____ Geste" (Gary Cooper adventure film)
16. Carrie Fisher role
17. Feel remorse
18. Title role for Robin Williams
21. French water
22. Egyptian goddess of fertility
23. Service mail drop: abbr.
26. "Armageddon" actress Tyler
28. Word with stool or ladder
31. 1991 Robin Williams movie
35. _____ Turturro of "Angie"
36. Grafton of mystery
37. Guess from the airline capt.
38. American pastime stats
41. Diamond, maybe
43. Title role for Robin Williams
48. Pub drink
49. "Freebie and the _____"
50. Oscar winner for "The Killing Fields"
52. "Neither a borrower _____ a lender be"
53. Eleven, to un élève de français
54. Robin Williams drama, "_____ Poets Society"
55. Fearful cry
56. 1992 Robin Williams movie
57. Itches

DOWN

1. Popeye, slangily
2. Tabloid report
3. Sky light
4. Robin Williams flick, "_____ of D"
5. Cardinals' home
6. Stead
7. Suspect's story
8. Maps
9. Supermodel Brinkley
10. Robin Williams played a villain in "One _____ Photo"
11. Weapon for Hamlet
19. Mustachioed painter
20. Schuyler _____ in "Orange County"
23. One _____ time
24. Magnetic flux symbol
25. "Kung Pow: Enter the Fist" director Steve
27. DVD predecessor
29. Talking tree creature in "The Lord of the Rings"
30. Org. in "Tin Cup"
32. Card game with the 13 spades laid out
33. Levy and O'Neill
34. Old film projector part
39. Main monk
40. Dictator's assistant

42. Mork's partner
43. Seymour in "Somewhere in Time"
44. Succulent plant
45. Lacking clarity
46. "The Night of the Hunter" screenwriter James
47. Reddish-brown, as a horse
51. Rtes.

HOLLYWOOD PROM KING

ACROSS

1. Actress Perlman
5. Thank-you card subject
9. Fall back, as a tide
12. Timeless times
13. Sexy secretary in "The Producers"
14. Figure skater Asada
15. Brad Pitt movie with tagline "Mischief. Mayhem. Soap."
17. Pal, in Paris
18. Actor Baldwin in "The Departed"
19. First choice
20. Brad Pitt's co-star in "Mr. & Mrs. Smith"
25. Pop singer Lewis
26. River seen from Stratford
27. Brad Pitt flick, "Thelma _____ Louise"
28. Phoenix's birthplace
30. _____-fi
33. Caesar said it as he died
34. What Gidget rode
35. Futuristic Brad Pitt movie
40. 30 minutes, in football
41. Goku has one on "Dragon Ball Z"
42. Peripherals standard: abbr.
43. Brad Pitt's role in the "Ocean's" movies
48. Classic muscle car
49. Amount to be raised, maybe
50. Common household list
51. Use needle and thread
52. Emulate a bartender
53. Elitist, in a way

DOWN

1. Call maker: abbr.
2. *Polloi* preceder
3. Headed for the altar
4. Scarlett's infatuation
5. Name on expensive bags
6. Unwell
7. Reason for feeling unwell
8. Account at restaurant or bar, for example
9. Online message
10. Disney deer
11. Idaho's capital
16. Ringer?: abbr.
19. "Miami Vice" star Johnson
20. Puzzle solver's shout
21. Helen Prejean in "Dead Man Walking," for one
22. Old Testament book
23. Main blvd. in NYC
24. Little Men sequel, "_____ Boys"
28. Off-roader, for short
29. Fr. holy woman
30. Lolita star
31. 1987 biographical film, "_____ Freedom"
32. Hypothethicals
33. Will Ferrell comedy
34. Sidesteps
35. Brad Pitt and others, in "Snatch"
36. Throw away

37. Arm joint
38. Wolverine's playful cousin
39. Senatorial refusal
43. Missy Elliott's music
44. A *padre's numero*

45. "High Roller: The _____ Ungar Story"
46. Bother
47. Head, in slang

Answers on page 250.

THE FRESH PRINCE

ACROSS

1. Like a bug in a rug
5. Children's movie, "The Secret of _____"
9. "The Talented Mr. Ripley" star Jude
12. Hawaii's coffee belt
13. Approving answer
14. Drink that may accompany fish and chips
15. 2007 Will Smith movie
17. Those who know a lot about anat.
18. Jennifer Lopez-Richard Gere flick, "_____ We Dance?"
19. 2004 Will Smith movie
21. Jodie Foster movie, "_____ Island"
23. Terminate
24. 2008 Will Smith movie
27. Grimm beastie
31. Article in the "Montreal Gazette"?
32. Actress Hasso
35. "Underworld" director Wiseman
36. Parts to tie
38. 1995 Will Smith movie
40. Quebec water
43. Sorvino of "WiseGirls"
44. 2008 Will Smith movie, "Seven _____"
47. Swanky dos
50. Will Smith's musical genre
51. Will Smith's "The Pursuit of _____"
54. "Well, what's this?!"
55. Watch like a lecher
56. Annoyed comment
57. 1987's "Empire of the _____"
58. Big execs
59. Price tag qualification

DOWN

1. Hits the slopes
2. Flood survivor
3. Like some spacecraft
4. Of France
5. Christmas drink
6. Pres. after Harry
7. Excessively excited
8. Many-headed mythical monster
9. Gentle sort
10. Actor Ray in "We're No Angels"
11. 1999 Will Smith movie, "Wild Wild _____"
16. "St. _____ Fire"
20. "Double Fantasy" artist
22. Elem. school class
24. Color
25. "The Sisterhood of the Traveling Pants" author Brashares
26. Org. Putin worked for
28. Poor winners
29. Fernando in "The French Connection"
30. Annapolis graduate's rank: abbr.
33. '60s war zone, briefly

34. Uplift intellectually or morally
37. Member of Cong.
39. Actress Vaccaro
41. Like some working groups
42. Gas bill factor
44. Some argument sides
45. Where Pearl City is

46. "Once _____ a Time in America"
48. Morales of "The Wonderful Ice Cream Suit"
49. Grounded planes
52. Group granted U.N. observer status in 1974
53. Latin foot

Answers on page 250.

INTERRUPTIONS

ACROSS

1. Newton cookie fruit
4. Mouth bone
7. Baseball stick
10. Wedding words
11. Metal from a mine
12. Quarterback Manning
13. Most satisfactory option
15. Morse code bit
16. "Now I see!"
17. Word from Scrooge
18. Think ahead
22. "_____ it or lose it"
23. Hacky Sack, basically
25. "_____ was saying . . ."
27. Constellation part
28. "I _____ your pardon"
29. Curved path
32. Baby's dinner neckwear
33. Weightlifter's apparatus
37. Bill with Washington's image
38. In the past
39. Take to court
40. X, in old Rome
41. Morning moisture
42. CNN founder Turner

DOWN

1. Little lie
2. Brainstorm
3. "Golly!"
4. Task
5. "_____ we there yet?"
6. Moist
7. Mattress critter
8. False name
9. 10% for the church
14. Sticky strip
19. _____ Vegas
20. Farm insect
21. Shaq's org.
23. London landmark
24. Saudi or Syrian
25. Monastery head
26. Paris's river
30. Take a break
31. Detective's find
33. Wicked
34. Get older
35. Line of theater seats
36. Had followers

Answers on page 250.

IT'S SPRING!

ACROSS

1. JC Penney rival
6. Outer ear cleaner
10. Taiwan's capital
11. Tall vases or coffee dispensers
12. Get to one's destination
13. Tiny bit
14. Scottish denials
15. Driver's 180-degree reversal
16. Alternate to a polo
19. Tiny bit
20. Anti-narcotics org.
21. July follower: abbr.
24. Apple product
28. 100 bucks, in slang
30. Golf scores
32. Skunk's defense
33. Darwin's _____ of evolution
35. Waiting place
36. Church talk
37. June 6, 1944 (WW II date)
38. Cyber messages

DOWN

1. 24 _____ gold
2. Bogs down
3. Gorilla-like
4. Gun an engine
5. Make a knot
6. Give up on a job
7. Rainbow fish
8. Prefix with mural
9. Mind your _____ Q's
10. Bronzed from sunning
15. Arizona neighbor
17. "If ___ before . . ."
18. Bodybuilder's unit
21. "Feed _____, starve . . ."
22. Reversed, as a word-processing error
23. _____ wild goose chase
25. Soap _____ (daytime serial)
26. Actress Watts
27. Old Hollywood's Flynn
29. Deuce beater in cards
31. Antonym's opposite: abbr.
33. Mao _____-tung
34. Sewn skirt edge

Answers on page 250.

IT'S SPRING!

ACROSS

1. Big, heroic stories, such as "Lord of the Rings"
6. Nodded off
11. Courtroom event
12. Join together, like states
13. Spring
15. Spider's work
16. "Enchanted" girl in a 2004 movie
20. One who hands out poker cards
25. Spring
27. "The Addams Family" uncle
28. Former husbands or wives
29. Cheering word
31. Spring
39. "Once upon _____ ..."
40. Pizza or burger topping
41. Pastry for Homer Simpson
42. "Glory be _____ ..."

DOWN

1. And so forth: abbr.
2. Paid athlete
3. Three in Roman numerals
4. Baseball's Ripken
5. Like a snail's pace
6. More idiotic
7. "We're number _____!"
8. Pimple
9. Pilot's announcement of arrival time: abbr.
10. VP Biden's state: abbr.
14. Indiana Jones hats
16. Santa's helper
17. Big name in jeans
18. _____ Vegas
19. Tenant's one-room place: abbr.
21. Sense of wonder
22. Not at all strict
23. Before, to a poet
24. Ave. relatives
26. Weasel-like pet
30. Owl sound
31. Chewing gum glob
32. From _____ Z
33. The _____ Man from "The Wizard of Oz"
34. Tall, flightless bird
35. 7-DOWN in Spanish
36. Manipulate, as an election
37. Dove sound
38. Finish

Answers on page 251.

GEOGRAPHY RIDDLES

ACROSS

1. Morning times: abbr.
4. Omelet ingredient
7. America's "Uncle"
10. Haul a wrecked car
11. Zodiac lion
12. Stretch out, or stretch the truth
13. This number divided by itself equals itself
14. A U.S. state that fits this setup: ___ ___ O R ___ ___ A
16. Very angry
17. Biblical garden place
18. Hockey surface
19. Cannon sound
22. The "I" in this U.S. state separates two words that are opposites of each other
27. Has a meal
28. "Just _____ thought!"
29. U.S. state with a panhandle: abbr.
32. Tennis match part
33. U.S. state that fits this setup: ___ ___ O R ___ ___ A
37. Woman's name, or abbr. of Boise's state
38. Streets: abbr.
39. Raggedy girl doll
40. Catholic sister
41. Suffix for fast, high, and strong
42. Cloud's place
43. Photo _____ (White House events)

DOWN

1. Kind of clock, number, or energy
2. Where Monte Carlo is
3. Where Stockholm is
4. North Pole helper
5. Hair-styling stuff
6. Sticky stuff
7. Dove into a base
8. White House helper
9. Nasty
15. "Do _____ fa sol ..."
19. "Who Wants to _____ Millionaire"
20. Halloween's month: abbr.
21. NFL "fifth quarters": abbr.
23. Far's opposite
24. Gambling house
25. Entirely gone, like car fuel
26. Tennessee's NFL team
29. Shrek, for example
30. Classic sneakers
31. Didn't win
34. Car fuel
35. Pen filler
36. "... have you _____ wool?"

Answers on page 251.

UPLIFTING MELODIES

ACROSS

1. Pasta or potato, to an athlete
5. Syllables of triumph
9. Air rifle ammo
12. Off in the distance
13. Mosque official
14. "A mouse!"
15. Thin material for book pages
17. Pub offering
18. Early game in a tournament
19. Enroll
21. Always, in poetry
22. Ens' preceders
24. Jefferson, religiously
25. Author Calvino
27. Old soda
28. Uplifting melodies?
32. Melissa Etheridge's "_____ Am"
33. "Iliad" and "Odyssey", e.g.
34. Mess participant
36. Dry, as wine
37. Golf tutor
40. Dug
42. One waited for in vain
44. Giant outfielder Mel
45. Unsportsmanlike conduct
47. "The Facts of Life" actress Charlotte
48. Gray matter output
49. Treater's phrase
50. ALF
51. C&W crooner Vince
52. Student woe

DOWN

1. _____ diem (seize the day)
2. Burning up
3. Andretti's auto
4. Composer Jacques
5. Pippen, to Jordan, once
6. Part of a sound system
7. Coin stampers
8. Roll-on brand
9. Freshman caps of old
10. John of "The Blues Brothers"
11. Doubter
16. Madonna portrayal
20. Biological ranking
23. Feeds, in a sty
25. Vine-covered
26. Eastern
28. Trash on the street, say
29. Accepted eagerly, as a chance
30. Subjects of wills
31. Hatfield enemy
35. Use a shovel again
37. Get on the horn with
38. Inn offerings
39. Young hooter
41. Conn of "Benson"
43. Kiddie-lit canine
46. Theologian's subj.

Answers on page 251.

COMPOSE YOURSELF

ACROSS

1. Switchblade
5. Nod
9. Corvine cry
12. Jennifer, on "WKRP in Cincinnati"
13. Roosevelt's Scottie
14. Copy
15. Summit
16. Circulate
17. Move up and down
18. Composer's phone call result?
21. Play performed with wooden masks
22. Crumb
25. Top flyer
28. Supper starter
31. Noisy return
32. Composer's trip ending?
35. Cellist's direction
36. Turf cover
37. Shoddy publication
38. Whale variety
40. CompuServe, e.g.
42. Composer's game?
48. Arafat's group: abbr.
50. Soft cheese
51. Singer Guthrie
52. Traffic trouble
53. Poker buy-in
54. "_____ and Stitch"
55. Actor Jack on "Barney Miller"
56. Suffices
57. Unassuming

DOWN

1. Chunk of concrete
2. Their Creator was Tawa, the Sun Spirit
3. Don Juan's mother
4. One of Santa's reindeer
5. Branch
6. Hindu goddess
7. Sleep like _____
8. Signs of fatigue
9. Aerial tramway
10. Private address?
11. What a browser browses
19. Reggae singer Peter
20. Take down _____
23. Green pet?
24. Movie ape
25. "Down with," in Dijon
26. Be a kvetch
27. Pilate's words
29. She played the Bride in "Kill Bill"
30. Orbital points
33. Circle dance
34. Lhasa ____
39. "Excuse me!"
41. One in a Book of 150
43. First Bond film with Sean Connery
44. Nick at ____
45. New York border lake
46. Women's magazine
47. Crackpot
48. Nightwear
49. Asian ethnic group

Answers on page 251.

FROZEN EXILE

ACROSS

1. Thick carpet
5. Gillette razor brand
9. Letter addenda: abbr.
12. Matador's opponent
13. Keogh alternatives
14. From _____ Z (completely)
15. With all sincerity
17. "Neither fish _____ fowl"
18. Attack like a lion
19. Where the elated walk
21. City in the Ruhr valley
22. Fine leather
24. Compete in cars
26. Bandleader Artie
27. Send some cads to the Arctic?
32. Teen outbreak
33. City north of Anaheim
34. Hockey's _____ Cup
36. Mural artist Rivera
41. Storage rack
42. Swindler
43. Folk rock's _____ DiFranco
44. Ignite
47. Rep. foe
48. First name in fashion
49. Bone by the radius
50. Language ending
51. Eye closers
52. Playwright Simon

DOWN

1. Fence bridger
2. Puts an edge on
3. Geometry calculations
4. Flip out
5. "Isn't" informal?
6. Three for Sophia
7. Dorm VIPs
8. Millionaire on the *Titanic*
9. Grand style
10. Impassive
11. Woes
16. Travis of country music
20. Carrot on a snowman, for example
22. Host Povich
23. Fairy tale menace
25. Dressing gown
27. Gush
28. Pump figures
29. Way to stop
30. What libraries do
31. Sported
35. Disinfectant brand
37. Just kidding around
38. Griffith of the ring
39. "With parsley," on some menus
40. Cager Shaq
42. Wheel teeth
45. Cotton gin inventor Whitney
46. Cable king Turner

1	2	3	4	■	5	6	7	8	■	9	10	11
12				■	13				■	14		
15				16					■	17		
18						■	■	19	20			
21					■	22	23					
■	■	■	■	24	25			■	26			
27	28	29	30				31					
32				■	33				■	■	■	■
34				35			■	36	37	38	39	40
41					■	■	42					
43			■	44	45	46						
47			■	48				■	49			
50			■	51				■	52			

MLB RECORDS

ACROSS

1. Former home run king McGwire
5. On the __ (fleeing)
8. Cy Young has the most in MLB history
12. _____ vera (natural soother)
13. Billy Martin's retired uniform number
14. Square footage
15. Barry Bonds has the most in MLB history
17. Doe's baby
18. Muscle definition
19. King Kong, e.g.
21. Cut and paste
24. Coffee allure
28. _____ Mitzvah
30. Fly like an eagle
32. _____ capita income
33. Joe DiMaggio has the longest in MLB history
36. "Much _____ About Nothing"
37. Fig. on a baseball card
38. Industrious bug
39. Like an extra-inning game
41. Put through a sieve
43. Prankster's missile
45. Right-hand person
48. "Ali __ and the Forty Thieves"
51. Walter Johnson had the most in MLB history
55. Former Tigers shortstop and manager Trammell
56. "For _____ a jolly..."
57. Granny
58. Pete Rose has the most in MLB history
59. Vote of assent
60. Grand _____ (four-run shot)

DOWN

1. _____-jongg
2. "Thanks _____!"
3. Cowboys quarterback Tony
4. Most perceptive
5. Manager Piniella
6. Raggedy doll (female)
7. Flat formation
8. Necco candy piece
9. Nest-egg letters
10. _____ York Knights ("The Natural" team)
11. _____ Diego Chicken (baseball mascot debuting in 1977)
16. Rose's color, for most of his career
20. Go splitsville
22. "Money _____ everything!"
23. Frat party wear
25. Play game one of a series
26. Vegan's no-no
27. Genesis boat
28. _____ one's time (wait)
29. "This must weigh _____!"
31. Italian bubbly

33. _____ trick (hockey feat)
34. Words of understanding
35. GI food
40. Stretches across
42. Jack Sprat's taboo
44. Visibly pale
46. Like a Jekyll-Hyde personality
47. Sicilian spewer

48. Outburst from Scrooge
49. He dethroned Foreman
50. Roy Hobbs's "Wonderboy"
52. Front end of a bray
53. Springsteen's "Born in the
    _____"
54. Baseball great Crawford or
    Jethroe

PLAY BALL!

ACROSS

1. _____ Ruth, "The Sultan of Swat"
5. Once around the track
8. _____ out (is retired on an easy fly)
12. "I smell _____!" (words from the suspicious)
13. Quarterback Manning
14. Kind of sax
15. Accompanied by
16. Time for a class picnic, perhaps
18. Regret greatly
20. Many a Little League coach
21. Bullring cry
22. Bus station
26. Flow back, like the tide
28. Stand in line, e.g.
32. In _____ straits
33. Hawaiian floral wreath
34. Homeless cat or dog
36. Ball supporter for young Little Leaguers
37. Disappear, like snow
39. "A _____ coincidence . . ."
40. Grifter
41. Howard of satellite radio
43. Baseball bat wood
45. Corn serving
47. Squares, circles, etc.
50. Small motorboat
54. Like sports telecasts, often
55. Randy Johnson, "The Big _____"
56. Cool _____ cucumber
57. Very top
58. _____ up (does a relief stint in a blowout game)
59. Tampa Bay player
60. Declare untrue

DOWN

1. Cry like a baby
2. Operatic solo
3. Auto seen around Gotham City
4. "I Love Lucy" neighbor _____ Mertz
5. _____ on base (inning stat)
6. Boxing great Muhammad
7. The _____ Piper
8. Like an umpire's chest protector
9. Casey Stengel, "The _____ Professor"
10. School org.
11. _____ sauce (Chinese restaurant condiment)
17. Young fellow
19. Anchorman's broadcast
23. Device used to tune an instrument
24. Nabisco cookie since 1912
25. Typical MTV viewer
26. Shade trees
27. Red veggie
29. $20s dispenser: abbr.
30. Ill temper
31. _____ and feather (old punishment)

35. Slangy assent
38. Rewards for doggie tricks
42. Throw out on an attempted steal, say
44. Fare for dieters
46. Crowd sound
47. Hang around

48. All tied up
49. Alluring, like a supermodel
50. Pirate's quaff
51. _____, dos, tres
52. Beat, but barely
53. World Baseball Classic team

Answers on page 252.

WHIP IT!

ACROSS

1. Word on many planes
4. Boat with an open hold
8. Soap _____ (bathroom grime)
12. Actress Zadora
13. Dear _____ (advice column)
14. "High Noon" marshal
15. "I.Q." role for Matthau
17. Bear seen at night?
18. She played Indy's love Marion Ravenwood
20. Disney film set in China
23. Flow blockage
24. Busy
25. "Soul _____" (1997 film about family)
28. She played Indy's enemy Irina Spalko
34. Jane played by Joan Fontaine
35. Black-and-white cookie
36. Spheres
39. Star of the 1929 film "The Mysterious Dr. Fu Manchu"
40. Indy's sidekick in "Indiana Jones and the Temple of Doom"
44. _____ doble (dance played at bullfights)
45. Fanatical
49. Lacking moisture
50. Ancient Jedi master
51. Creeping plant
52. Lots
53. Border for the Holy Grail in "Indiana Jones and the Last Crusade"
54. Actress Ruby or Frances

DOWN

1. King Kong, for one
2. Maj. Charles Emerson Winchester _____ on TV's "M*A*S*H"
3. Jogged
4. Peter Stormare's role in "Constantine"
5. Biological org. with the FDA
6. Theatrical or ad award
7. "The Absent-Minded Professor" actor Keenan
8. "Indiana Jones and the Kingdom of the Crystal _____"
9. Monte _____
10. Still soft, as wet cement
11. Malicious
16. Emulate Sonja Henie
19. "Thunderstruck" group
20. Indy's friend who worked for MI6
21. Actress Hagen
22. On fire
25. Jeff Goldblum sci-fi film, with "The"
26. Paddle
27. "The Big Red _____" (1980 war film)
29. "My _____ Friend's Wedding"
30. Wrestling moves

31. Distinct period in history
32. "The _____ Command-ments"
33. "Dracula" director Browning
36. Mitchell's "Gone with the Wind" protagonist
37. Needed by some virtuosos
38. Indy's comrade in "Raiders of the Lost Ark"

39. "Barry Lyndon" star
40. Most e-mail from deposed Nigerian princes
41. Rogers and Orbison
42. Woodwind instrument
43. Meat-inspecting agcy.
46. Wicked boy in "Toy Story"
47. "Grease" actress Arden
48. Easter egg coloring

Answers on page 252.

IN THE LEAD

ACROSS

1. Separated
6. Evil act
9. When the sun is out
12. Enjoy unhurriedly
13. Gardening tool
14. George Gershwin's brother
15. Country leader
17. Stimpy's cartoon pal
18. Like a barber pole
19. Make a small adjustment
21. Slippery tree?
22. Voting group
23. Money
26. Perfumed
29. Cigar remnant
30. Mom's mate
31. Hockey great Bobby
32. Where a liner may put in
35. Atomizer output
37. Debt promises
38. Waitress on "Alice"
39. Italian actress Sophia
41. Loud wailing
45. Volt-ampere
46. Orchestra leader
48. By way of
49. Fleecy female
50. The others
51. Phanerozoic, e.g.
52. Participate in a quilting bee
53. Beekeepers' product

DOWN

1. Venomous snakes
2. Segment
3. Declare
4. More cheerful
5. Three-bagger
6. Storage structure
7. Charged particle
8. Stinging plant
9. Film leader
10. Zone
11. Pull hard
16. Rep. opponent
20. Was victorious
22. A train?
23. _____ Vegas
24. Employ
25. Meeting leader
26. Rested in a chair
27. Historical period
28. Free of moisture
30. ER figures
33. "The Purloined Letter" writer
34. Fractions of a pound
35. Mystery solver
36. Protection from the rain
38. Gave a dinner to
39. Dallas airport
40. Indiana neighbor
41. Hitchcock's "The Man Who _____ Too Much"
42. Take _____ the lam
43. Small winning margin
44. Western writer Zane
47. Have a tab

Answers on page 252.

THE CROSSWORD WITHOUT A THEME

ACROSS

1. Almost closed
5. Caviar source
8. Stringed instrument
12. The skin manufactures it when exposed to sunlight
14. About
15. As an asset
17. V followers
18. Gent
19. Offerer of moral lessons
20. Cook in the microwave, slangily
21. Summer center?
22. Mock
25. City vehicle
26. Solver's exclamation
29. Historic section of New Orleans
33. Beer container
34. British ending?
35. Slender amphibian
36. Cause perplexity in
37. Passats, e.g.
39. Tenochtitlán dweller
42. Forest mom
43. _____ Olivos, California
46. Contributed, as a comment
49. Longtime smoker?
50. Yogurt content
51. Speaks
52. Athlete's week off, perhaps
53. Big celebration

DOWN

1. Confess
2. Cause of bad luck
3. Part of D.A.: abbr.
4. Enthusiastic cheer
5. Shred
6. Just
7. End of Juilliard's e-mail address
8. Firefighting equipment
9. Budget competitor
10. Make over
11. Kind of school
13. _____ Millions (lottery game)
16. Brazilian dance
20. Type of meditation
21. _____ de parfum
22. Home airport of JetBlue
23. "Where the Wild Things _____" (Sendak book)
24. Categorize
25. International distress signal
26. Attacked a hero, say
27. Attack with an ax
28. Exhibit material
30. Native of Bohemia
31. Cause of bad luck
32. M.D.'s coworkers
36. Robert Urich TV series
37. Able to produce sounds
38. Traveled
39. Bowls over
40. Greek letter
41. Very little

42. Climax of the Allied advance
43. Mussolini's money
44. R&B singer Redding
45. Former monarch of Iran
47. Kind of tide
48. Complex arrangement

1	2	3	4		5	6	7		8	9	10	11
12				13					14			
15							16				
17				18				19				
			20				21					
22	23	24				25				26	27	28
29				30	31				32			
33				34					35			
			36				37	38				
39	40	41				42				43	44	45
46				47			48			
49				50							
51				52				53			

CURRENT EVENTS

ACROSS

1. Some Japanese cartoons
6. Triangular sail
9. Water purity org.
12. Clutch, perhaps
13. Rare sighting
14. Tic follower
15. Deceptive advertising operation
18. Imitated a whale
19. Scouting pledge word
20. B.C. carnivore
21. _____ Paulo, Brazil
23. Movie pig
25. Kind of bar
27. Gives the green light to
30. Like some surveillance systems
33. Trill name on "Star Trek: Deep Space Nine"
34. Having no give
35. Dept. of Justice employee
36. Method
37. Coloring
39. Prosaic
42. Progress hamperer
45. Many a speedster
48. Bran source
49. Prefix with brow
50. Horned creature
51. Word before hill or jumper
52. Kettle and Bell
53. Jobs

DOWN

1. Police band calls: abbr.
2. First quarter moon effect
3. TV, slangily
4. Becomes due
5. Thrill
6. "High Crimes" actress
7. Conditional statements
8. Violin stick
9. Remark to a backstabber
10. Treaty
11. "_____ Breaky Heart"
16. Delivery service promise
17. Groom's reply
21. Skim along a surface
22. Publicize
23. They lead to E
24. Nouvelle Caledonie, e.g.
26. Possible post-ER stop
27. Film flubs
28. Model builder's purchase
29. Where slop is served
31. Greek H
32. Sacred composition
36. A question of identity
38. "That is"
39. Super Mario _____
40. Fuel tank problem
41. Play opener
42. Hitter's stats
43. Lift up the wrapping, perhaps
44. Miscalculates
46. Pirate's quaff
47. Recombinant _____

Answers on page 252.

THAT'S A HOT ONE

ACROSS

1. Mock
5. _____ homo
9. Agent 99's husband
12. Cruising, perhaps
13. Crowd noise
14. Penny portrait
15. Device using a magnetron
18. Early form of plastic
19. Gov't meat grader
20. Biblical site
21. Actress-turned-poker-player Tilly
23. Bushranger Kelly
25. Cleared course
29. Metal-lined fireplace
33. Overdue book fine
34. Uncooked
35. Don't dawdle
36. Netflix deliveries
39. Passing notice
42. Baked Alaska filling
46. Best in one's class
48. Deuce
49. Cry of mock horror
50. Bump into
51. Familiar
52. Stuns
53. Puts in

DOWN

1. Door section
2. Polo field?
3. Ate like a bird?
4. Dog or flop ending
5. Monroe's "The Seven Year Itch" co-star
6. Blazer
7. Alley Oop, e.g.
8. Before, in poetry
9. Dallas players, for short
10. Out for the night?
11. Lucy Lawless part
16. Spanish cheer
17. Word of obligation
22. Martians, e.g.
23. Organization covering 2 conferences
24. Baseball pitcher's stat
25. Dessert sometimes served a la mode
26. Went downhill
27. Actress Gardner
28. Ground hemlock
30. "Super duper!"
31. Col. Sanders's chain
32. "Don't dwell on the past"
36. Monopoly documents
37. Tape machine: abbr.
38. Excitement
39. Football great Graham
40. College football game name
41. Ubiquitous music player
43. Portion of tobacco
44. Like fine Scotch
45. Subway Series team
47. Word in a U.S. Marines slogan

Answers on page 252.

CROSSWORD

ACROSS

1. Not good
4. Old cloth used for dusting
7. Go _____ vacation
8. Word ending that means "sort of"
9. It holds back water in a river
12. Strange
13. Enjoy a winter sport
14. Cheer for a bullfighter
15. City in Florida
17. Tokyo's country
19. Number that appears on a penny
21. Geeky person
22. Monkey bars
25. Not straight
26. Distant
27. "Honesty _____ best policy"
29. It's poured over waffles
33. "Just _____ thought!"
34. Struck a match
36. Had a snack
37. "_____ you later, alligator!"
38. He runs a bar on "The Simpsons"
39. Sound made by a wood-pecker
40. Your and my
41. That lady

DOWN

1. Sound of an explosion
2. Me, myself, _____:
3. How a baby might say "father"
4. Moving up
5. Have a question
6. Letters after F
9. One of the Seven Dwarfs
10. _____ clock (item that can wake you up)
11. Heal
16. $\frac{1}{12}$ of a year
18. Really upset
20. One of Santa's assistants
22. _____ James (famous outlaw)
23. Remove a knot
24. Holiday with bunnies and eggs
25. Prejudice
28. Red Muppet
30. "Darn it!"
31. State with the Great Salt Lake
32. _____ Le Pew (cartoon skunk)
35. Paper that shows a debt

Answers on page 253.

THIS IS THE DAY

ACROSS

1. "Bam!"
4. 'Vette roof option
8. Self-satisfied
12. Lyric poem
13. Roll call response
14. Chopped liver spread
15. Sunrise devotion
18. Primps
19. Revolted
20. Mai _____ (cocktail)
21. Monthly rent outlay, e.g.: abbr.
22. Vehicle for school kids
25. Charged particle
27. Vaulted church recess
31. Siestas
35. Bean source of tofu
36. Medical care grp.
37. Feline pet
38. Sought elected office
41. Residential suffix
43. Draw, as football game
46. Powerful Greek deities
50. Factory guard, after closing time
52. Swiss painter Paul
53. Confederate General Robert _____
54. One _____ time
55. Witnessed
56. Actor Alan of "Shane"
57. Emulate a bunny

DOWN

1. Ceremonial splendor
2. Smell
3. "The Way We _____"
4. Where things seem to disappear into
5. Stress
6. Assn.
7. Enliven
8. Michigan State athlete
9. BLT spread
10. Sport _____ (family cars)
11. Actor Richard of "Pretty Woman"
16. Butterfly catcher's tool
17. Tach reading: abbr.
22. _____-relief (sculptural style)
23. ET's ride
24. Pig's digs
26. Japanese drama
28. Lobbyist employer, for short
29. Health club feature
30. Winter hrs. in Boston
32. Like pottery
33. Left out
34. Observed
39. Little island, in Britain
40. Staircase support
42. Archaic verb ending
43. Fountain pen fluids
44. Egypt's river
45. "The African Queen" screenwriter James

47. Asian nursemaid
48. Defense grp. since 1949
49. Click of the fingers
51. Apple pie _____ mode

PART OF A RAINBOW

ACROSS

1. North American deer
4. Opera highlight
8. Fish propellers
12. Pistol, e.g.
13. Neet competitor
14. Chess piece also called a castle
15. Jealous
18. Soothsayer
19. "Absolutely!"
20. Perched on
24. Ostrich cousins
28. Cookie-selling org.
31. Repulsive
33. _____ St. Vincent Millay (poet)
34. One in a U.S. military flight demonstration squadron
37. "A Death in the Family" author
38. "My word!"
39. Lamb's mom
40. "He's got the whole _____ in His hands"
42. Demonstrate
44. "_____ goes the weasel!"
46. Chance occurrences
50. Indoor ornamental plant
56. Part of speech
57. Hall of Fame pitcher Nolan
58. Employ
59. Barrel bottom bit
60. TV rooms, often
61. Cut the grass

DOWN

1. Hen's output
2. Tackle box item
3. Leg joint
4. Raggedy doll
5. Uncooked
6. A crowd, for Caesar?
7. Pretentiously cultural
8. Renew
9. Charged particle
10. Thanksgiving mo.
11. Cloud's site
16. Significant time period
17. That girl
21. Bathroom fixture
22. Make goo-goo eyes at
23. Outlet inserts
25. Competitive advantage
26. Once more
27. Mall attraction
28. Emulate a beaver
29. Starch-producing palm
30. Declare
32. Slangy affirmative
35. Sharp barking
36. "Much _____ About Nothing"
41. Physician, briefly
43. "Which person?"
45. Cowpoke's bud
47. College grad
48. Mexican money
49. Meal in a pot
50. "Furthermore . . ."
51. Not against

52. Regret
53. Comic Louis
54. Moving-day rental
55. Election winners

1	2	3		4	5	6	7		8	9	10	11
12				13					14			
15			16					17				
18							19					
			20	21	22	23		24		25	26	27
28	29	30		31			32		33			
34			35				36					
37					38					39		
40				41		42			43			
			44		45				46	47	48	49
50	51	52				53	54	55				
56					57					58		
59					60					61		

APPRECIATION

ACROSS

1. Ice cream treat
5. Ray of sun
9. "..._____ will be done . . ."
12. Wing-related
13. "Sad to say . . ."
14. _____ *polloi*
15. "You've pleased me, Pierre!"
18. Immeasurable period
19. Gun the engine
20. Yours and mine
21. Possesses
22. Grocery holder
24. Baghdad's land
27. Biological pouch
28. Fruity quaff
31. "You've pleased me enormously!"
35. Wall St. debut: abbr.
36. Luau memento
37. Classic 'Vette competitors
38. Keats wrote one on an urn
39. Coffee holder
41. Ancient Roman attire
44. Massage table murmur
45. Boxer once known as Clay
48. "You've pleased me, pal!"
52. Prepare to shoot
53. _____ gin fizz
54. Medicinal amount
55. "Mayday!"
56. Perfect Olympic scores, sometimes
57. Hold as an opinion

DOWN

1. Identical
2. Ersatz butter
3. Mend socks
4. Curved path
5. Innocent ones
6. Hgt.
7. Motorist's org.
8. East Lansing sch.
9. 10 C-notes
10. Sixty minutes
11. Puppy's noises
16. A Gershwin
17. Machine tooth
21. Mil. command posts
22. Sheepish remark?
23. Do something
24. Three on a sundial
25. Hit sharply
26. Latin 101 word
27. Hindu honorific
28. Toward the stern
29. Batman and Robin, e.g.
30. Golf great Ernie
32. Like many a "knock-knock" joke
33. "Golly!"
34. Breakfast staple
38. Feedbag morsel
39. Creates
40. Conversational stumbles
41. "_____the night before Christmas . . ."
42. Cleveland's state
43. Phys-ed rooms

44. Soon
45. Soothing plant
46. Suffer defeat
47. List element

49. FDR's successor
50. Pub offering
51. Do some sums

Answers on page 253.

NUMBER ONE AT THE BOX OFFICE

ACROSS

1. Blockhead
4. "The Man _____ Knew Too Much" (1956 Day drama)
7. "_____ Mia!" (2008 movie musical)
12. Frost
13. "Keep It Under Your _____" (song from Calamity Jane)
14. Cooked one's own goose?
15. Lions' home
17. Tilted to one side (British)
18. 1959 Day comedy
20. Script sections
22. Haw's partner
23. Greek war god
24. Moon Unit, to Dweezil
25. Submissions to literary agts.
28. 1961 Day comedy
32. Lamb's parent
33. Steve Case's company
34. Morales of "Fast Food Nation"
35. Employed pols
36. Crazy _____ (card game)
38. Costar in 18- and 28-ACROSS
41. Like some blockades
42. Bunch of golf events
45. Actress Dunne
46. "_____ for Two" (1950 Day film)
47. The old college _____
48. Goals for actors
49. Mork's home planet
50. Hurricane heading

DOWN

1. Factory super in "The Pajama Game"
2. Breeze through
3. Personal bugaboo
4. Entire
5. Yells "Taxi!," e.g.
6. Film director Preminger
7. Like Hammett's Falcon
8. George Peppard TV series, with "The"
9. Breakfast or brunch
10. "That Touch of _____" (1962 Day film)
11. Hill dweller
16. Shampooing instruction
19. Impulse
20. Result of a successful pitch
21. Losers eat this
24. The Sun
25. Effusive love letter
26. Ella's style of singing
27. Emulates Day in Caprice
29. Annoys
30. Thug's bludgeon
31. Engendered
35. "_____ help it!"
36. Gardener's tool
37. Singer-songwriter Chris
38. _____ avis
39. "Move _____ , Darling" (1963 Day film)
40. _____ no good
41. Tuck's partner
43. Grecian art object
44. Variety of whiskey

Answers on page 254.

NOT JUST A DEPARTMENT STORE SANTA

ACROSS

1. Sloop's sail
4. Scrambled _____
8. Soaks
12. Word before "Lobo" or "Grande" in movie titles
13. Five-peseta coin
14. Surveyor's chart
15. Do wrong
16. Russian sea
17. "_____ sow, so shall..."
18. He won an Oscar playing Kris Kringle in "Miracle on 34th Street"
21. Hand over
23. One of the Lennon Sisters
24. Stop using
26. *Chemin-de-_____*
27. Where Kris Kringle was employed
33. Spoil
34. Basketball game
35. In vogue
38. San _____ Capistrano
39. She played young Susan Walker in "Miracle on 34th Street"
42. Cool-sounding rapper
43. Nonkosher
44. McKellen who played Gandalf
47. Famed Phoenician port
48. Jack of "The Cannonball Run"
49. Taste
50. Sale condition
51. Physics unit
52. Stretch, with "out"

DOWN

1. PSAT takers, usually: abbr.
2. Three, to Tiberius
3. Arid
4. Dutch cheese
5. Venerable guide
6. Like Kris Kringle in "Miracle on 34th Street"
7. Foxhole occupant
8. Generate
9. Ashley of "Full House"
10. He played Fred Gailey in "Miracle on 34th Street"
11. Light submachine gun
19. _____ ringer
20. Brooks of country music
21. Des Moines hrs.
22. Author Umberto of Italy
25. Danger
28. Suggested
29. Charm
30. Profoundly knowledgeable
31. Top-secret org.
32. Top rating, often
35. Store featured in "Miracle on 34th Street"
36. Cheri of "Saturday Night Live"
37. Goes out with
39. Actress Talbot
40. Withdraw by degrees
41. "What's to become _____?" (words of despair)

45. Craft built for the Flood
46. Comic Louis

1	2	3		4	5	6	7		8	9	10	11
12				13					14			
15				16					17			
		18	19					20				
21	22					23						
24				25		26						
27				28				29	30	31	32
				33				34				
	35	36	37					38			
39						40	41				
42					43					44	45	46
47					48					49		
50					51					52		

PLAYING THE ROLE OF HEROES

ACROSS

1. Famous movie role for Heston
6. Donkey
9. Pro-gun group for which Heston was pres.
12. "Don't be such _____!" ("Stop bothering me!")
13. Current D. C. ballplayer
14. Have a bug
15. Volkswagen model
16. Bearded beast
17. Numbered hwy.
18. Famous scene in 30-ACROSS
21. Sword lilies, for short
22. Giant Manning
25. Amazon squeezer
26. Answer to "Who's there?"
30. Movie for which Heston won an Oscar in the title role
32. Heston and this friend were each president of the Screen Actors Guild
33. Ties tightly
34. Part of 29-DOWN
35. Trike rider
36. Rose pricker
38. Cause that Heston supported long before it became popular to do so in Hollywood
44. Overhead trains
45. Author LeShan
46. Lube anew

48. Sliced dessert
49. Break a commandment
50. Vintage violin
51. Foe and also friend to Heston's character in a "Planet" movie
52. Sen. Kennedy
53. Art class job for Heston in his lean, early days

DOWN

1. USAF rank
2. Energy cartel acronym
3. Green who played Doctor Evil's son
4. "¿Cómo _____ usted?"
5. Heston was one
6. Namibia neighbor
7. Sleigh driver
8. More solidly built
9. Drug bust cop
10. Communion, for one
11. Pub quaff
19. Composer Stravinsky
20. Cinematic pooch
22. _____ and flow
23. Oahu garland
24. Country lodge
25. Thickest and fullest, like eyebrows
27. NYPD rank
28. Former Chinese leader
29. Med. specialty
31. It shows a very clear image
32. Mumbai royal
34. Gofer's job

37. Tune from the past
38. Movie excerpt
39. "That's clear now"
40. Fat unit
41. Prefix with globin

42. Tailless amphibian
43. Set of Web pages
44. Clean Air Act org.
47. Rap's _____ Kim

Answers on page 254.

THE APATOW EMPIRE

ACROSS

1. Diamond corner
5. Herding dog's name
9. Roman robes
14. Strong ___ ox
15. "The Clan of the ___ Bear"
16. Wide awake
17. Mailed
18. Drive the getaway car, e.g.
19. Actor Bridges
20. She was Alison Scott in "Knocked Up"
23. Budding actress
24. Tech support caller
25. Helping hand
26. "___ Kleine Nachtmusik"
28. Patient remark?
31. Milky gemstones
34. Mitchell's plantation
35. Bake sale holder, often
36. 2006 Will Ferrell hit produced by Apatow
40. Vinaigrette ingredient
41. Reign
42. Burial place
43. Pointy shoe wearer
44. Go out with
45. OSS successor
46. Portent
48. Is unable to grasp, as a point
52. 1999 NBC series produced by Apatow
55. Dryly witty
56. Soothing succulent
57. Glassmaker's need
58. Actress Taylor of "The Nanny"
59. Catcher's glove
60. "The ___ Reader"
61. Beef on the hoof
62. Nice summers?
63. Falls behind

DOWN

1. Soaks in the sun
2. "Have ___!" (inviting words)
3. Red suit wearer
4. Hold spellbound
5. Quaking in one's boots
6. Nun's wear
7. Like half the integers
8. Tennis player Sampras
9. "Honor Thy Father" author
10. Kukla and Fran's partner
11. Earth science
12. Reactive radical
13. Part of E.S.T.: abbr.
21. "I Still See ___" (Paint Your Wagon tune)
22. Spicy cuisine
26. Philadelphia player
27. "Dies ___ "(Latin hymn)
29. Internet address starter
30. "And ___ thou slain the Jabberwock?"
31. Native Oklahoman
32. Kid's beach toy
33. Start of the Musketeers' motto

34. Germanic: abbr.
37. Wet one's whistle
38. Cake topping
39. Like one who's been rescued
44. Casino figure
45. West Point team
47. Brawl
48. Big bill

49. Simmons rival
50. Just managing, with "out"
51. _____ Park, Colorado
52. Guitar ridge
53. Matching
54. Landed (on)
55. Kildare and Zhivago: abbr.

Answers on page 254.

"LUCY, I'M HOME!"

ACROSS

1. Arnaz's country of origin
5. Maple fluid
8. TV network of "I Love Lucy"
11. Newspaper page
12. Gator tail?
13. Cry of wonder
14. "_____ boy!"
15. Arnaz feature on the "Walk of Fame"
16. Wonder
17. Movie on which Lucy met Arnaz
20. By a hair
21. Drs.' org.
24. Bad grades
25. *Coup d'_____*
29. Signature song of this performer
31. Production company founded by Lucille Ball and Arnaz
33. Make airtight
34. One-one, e.g.
35. Utmost
36. Second half of a phrase about not worrying
39. Arnaz's character on "I Love Lucy"
45. Oscars host Stewart
46. Middle East hot spot
47. Peter Pan pursuer
48. Perform
49. Transgress
50. French girlfriend
51. Studio that made 17-ACROSS
52. Used a chair
53. What Arnaz led

DOWN

1. Tower in San Francisco
2. _____ no good (seeking trouble)
3. Smooch, in 1-ACROSS
4. First man
5. Mythical Pan, and others
6. Old saying
7. Hazard
8. Energy source
9. Violinists' needs
10. Any ship
15. Military mix-up
18. A son of 4-DOWN
19. Deli breads
21. Tummy muscles
22. West of old Hollywood
23. Attys.' org.
26. Director Burton
27. Miss. neighbor
28. Monkey suit, in short
30. Emmy-winning Baldwin
31. "Start eating!"
32. Fair-hiring org.
34. Despot
37. "Prelude to _____" (Meg Ryan movie)
38. Site of Damascus
39. "30 _____" (30-DOWN TV show).
40. "_____ the Woods" (Sond-

224

heim musical)
41. Moby-Dick pursuer
42. Capital of *Italia*

43. Bump off
44. Signed off on
45. Pickle holder

Answers on page 255.

FOOTSTEPS

ACROSS

1. "Drat!"
5. Air-rifle ammo
8. Stitched
12. North Carolina college
13. Ooh and _____
14. Aesop's also-ran
15. 1989 Douglas flick, with "The"
18. Simple bed
19. Olympian Jesse
20. *La _____ vita*
23. Cafeteria carrier
25. Asian nurse
26. Dregs
27. 180° from NNW
30. 1992 Douglas flick
33. Picnic invader
34. "Thanks _____!"
35. "_____ me!"
36. Boris Godunov, for one
37. Brouhaha
38. Holler
41. Dr. bloc
42. 1998 Douglas flick, with "A"
48. At one time, at one time
49. Bauxite, e.g.
50. Heavy cart
51. Romances
52. Opposite of bellum
53. Arid

DOWN

1. Drops on blades
2. According to
3. Scand. country
4. Potato dumplings
5. Fabric stuffing
6. "_____ humbug!"
7. "_____ Cried" (1962 hit)
8. Ostentatious
9. Alleviate
10. Small songbird
11. 1987 Costner role
16. Antagonist
17. Certain tribute
20. "The Aba _____ Honeymoon"
21. Arab League member
22. Bringing up the rear
23. Andrea Bocelli, for one
24. What's left over
26. Actress Kedrova
27. Bygone blade
28. Read quickly
29. *Raison d'_____*
31. Untouchables, e.g.
32. Checkpoint requests
36. Massachusetts university
37. Dallas sch.
38. Erupt
39. Deli offering
40. Approximately
41. Financial pg.
43. Bluecoat
44. "La la" preceder
45. Dr. of rap
46. Ring bearer, maybe
47. "The Catcher in the _____"

Answers on page 255.

"SHE DID IT THE HARD WAY"

ACROSS

1. *Amo, amas*, _____
5. Outlawed spray
8. Shells, e.g.
12. Speed Racer's car
14. Seven-day period
15. 1956 Davis film, with "The"
17. Order between "ready" and "go"
18. Lindley of "The Ropers"
19. Moisten the turkey
22. Campus place
24. Largest continent
25. Disadvantages
26. Trygve's successor
29. Davis role in "Now, Voyager"
32. Modeling line?
33. Currier's partner
34. Golfer's club choice
35. TV music marketer
36. _____ Foods, maker of Little Debbie cakes
37. Tati's "ta ta"
40. Collapsible bed
41. Movie in which Davis played Catherine the Great
47. Middle Eastern sultanate
48. Things to be proven
49. Hair quality
50. It's heard before "gee"
51. "Thank _____ Lucky Stars" (1943 all-star musical that included Davis)

DOWN

1. Cable channel for film devotees
2. Cry of farm young
3. Play a role
4. 1952 Davis film
5. Go easy on the calories
6. Netflix rental
7. Afternoon drink
8. Terrible
9. Anthroplogist Margaret
10. Prime Minister elected in March 1969
11. Cajun staple
13. Let loose
16. Fake
19. One of the Three B's
20. _____ Stadium in Queens
21. Land of Chang and Eng
22. Davis starred in the pilot for this TV series
23. Colonial critters?
25. Shoreline recess
26. 1939 Davis melodrama, with 31-DOWN
27. Skin lotion ingredient
28. Hackman of "Unforgiven"
30. Started smoking
31. See 26-DOWN
35. Oft-killed "South Park" character
36. Magic charm
37. "Get _____" (1958 hit song)
38. Major ending

39. "It made me sick when _____ to let ya kiss me": Davis in "Of Human Bondage"
40. Bass, for one
42. Gave in to the munchies
43. 14 and up, for short
44. Hero of the "Matrix" trilogy
45. Down Under bird
46. Kazakhstan, once: abbr.

FROM CIRCUS TO STAR

ACROSS

1. TV alien
4. Car thief's bane
9. Apple seed
12. _____ polloi
13. Excessive enthusiasm
14. "_____ be a monkey's uncle!"
15. 1941 Grant drama
17. Pakistani president, 1978–88
18. Deplore
19. Egg carton count
21. 1941 Grant melodrama
25. Ripens
26. Story
27. Candidate for day care
28. Upside down lower-case "e"
30. Catch
33. Swing in the breeze
34. Wolf, in Juarez
35. 1940 Grant comedy
40. "None but the Lonely Heart" director
41. Resistance figures
42. Golf average
43. 1958 Grant comedy
48. Fraternal letter
49. Surrealist Max
50. Grant's employer in "Notorious"
51. Hither and _____
52. Shooting sport
53. Membership requirement, often

DOWN

1. Physical responses
2. Mae West role in "She Done Him Wrong"
3. Stocking material
4. Accord
5. Prepares new sneakers
6. Nickname of the young Darth Vader
7. Notorious setting, briefly
8. De Klerk's successor
9. Popular take-out order
10. Coming-clean words
11. Grant's pursuer in "North by Northwest"
16. Gives a bad review to
20. "Room for _____ More" (1952 Grant movie)
21. First Lady Nixon
22. Something to stroke
23. Gas additive
24. Not cooked
28. Rustles
29. Parker's responsibility
30. Dozes a bit
31. Attorneys' org.
32. Lad
33. Snorkel's rank: abbr.
34. Branch
35. The Rubbles' family pet on "The Flintstones"
36. Boise's state
37. Bird in the finch family
38. "All That Jazz" subject
39. Scarlett's love

44. Where Mork and Mindy honeymooned
45. French article
46. Presidential nickname
47. Cravat

1	2	3		4	5	6	7	8		9	10	11
12				13						14		
15			16							17		
		18						19	20			
21	22					23	24					
25						26						
27					28	29				30	31	32
			33						34			
35	36	37				38	39					
40						41						
42				43	44	45					46	47
48				49						50		
51				52						53		

Answers on page 255.

BBC MD

ACROSS

1. Most Super Bowl MVPs, for short
4. Stick
8. Landed
12. Have lunch
13. Roman attire of old
14. Actor Diego of "Milk"
15. Modern ID verifier
16. Abu Dhabi denizen
17. Long, limp, straight
18. Antisocial TV character played by Laurie
21. *Modus operandi*
22. A violinist might use one or take one
23. "Jabberwocky" opener
25. Small bit
27. Curative place
30. Bumbling TV character played in the 1990s by Laurie
33. Middle muscles
34. Try to learn a semester's worth of lessons in one night
35. Potato tablemate
36. Meadow
37. Ambulance chaser's exhortation
38. Movie character whose adoptive father was played by Laurie
44. Check
45. Hawkeyes' home
46. Flight sched. info
48. Skin outburst
49. Brief passing words?
50. What Laurie did in competition
51. Hoodwink
52. All's opposite
53. Show that launched Eddie Murphy, briefly

DOWN

1. Concluding letters
2. Screen-door sound
3. George Lucas classic
4. Not natural, as theater
5. Benicio Del _____
6. Seaweed derivative
7. 1987 Diane Keaton comedy
8. Give the O.K. to
9. Maui feast
10. Respites for the road-weary
11. Confiscate
19. Eden-to-Nod direction
20. _____ sapiens
23. Not on the TV sched. yet
24. Flycatcher?
25. Ventilator's job
26. Old Pan Am rival
27. Super Bowl XIV champs
28. Potpie veggie
29. Pop or op follower
31. Bakery worker
32. Moralist's target
36. Paint base choice
37. North Dakota or North Carolina, e.g.
38. Overthrown leader of Iran

39. Lunch with a crunch
40. Forearm bone
41. "Me and You and a Dog Named Boo" singer
42. Champion's cry

43. School attended by Laurie
47. Piercing tool

1	2	3		4	5	6	7		8	9	10	11
12				13					14			
15				16					17			
	18		19					20				
		21					22					
23	24				25	26				27	28	29
30				31					32			
33				34					35			
			36					37				
38	39	40				41	42				43	
44					45					46		47
48				49					50			
51				52					53			

Answers on page 256.

A SUCCESSFUL SMILE

ACROSS

1. Cookout letters
4. Leslie Caron film
8. Oliver Stone biopic
11. Gary's role in "The Pride of the Yankees"
12. "Star Wars" android Artoo _____
13. "_____ you nuts?"
14. Wonder
15. Ferrera's film debut, with 26-ACROSS
17. Dogcatcher's quarry
19. Actor Ed of "Daniel Boone"
20. North Pole products
21. They're checked outside bars
24. Tennis player Arthur
26. See 15-ACROSS
29. Improve, as cheese
32. Big knives
33. Ones with clout
34. "The _____ of the Traveling Pants" (Ferrera movie)
37. Explorer Hernando de _____
38. Canine cry
39. "Law & Order: SVU" costar
43. Gambler's city
45. It may be seria or buffa
46. Former Ferrera TV series
50. Put down, slangily
51. Hodges of the Dodgers
52. Flynn of swashbucklers
53. Emulate Ferrera
54. Whack weeds
55. June to June, say
56. "The Illustrated Man" author Bradbury

DOWN

1. Trumpet or dynamite sound
2. Honor, in a way
3. Express doubt about
4. "The Fall Guy" star Majors
5. "Give _____ rest"
6. "Ha ha," online
7. Waterloo setting
8. King of Scotland, 1567–1625
9. Top off
10. Documentarian Burns
12. In need of irrigation
16. Poet Khayyám
18. Pokémon protagonist
21. Ebony counterpart of song
22. City in India
23. Beat out on a newsbeat
25. Suffix with baron or count
27. Vigoda of "The Godfather"
28. Military supporter, for short
29. Donkey
30. Fashion designer Armani
31. Actress Winwood
35. "West Side Story" beau
36. Quick swim
40. Chest material
41. Susan Lucci's role on "All My Children"
42. "Yum!"
44. Follow instructions

45. Popeye's love
46. "Get that away from me!"
47. Before, to Byron
48. Ditty bit
49. Rocky peak

ANSWERS

Questionable Tunes (pages 4-5)

```
ATLAS   ABBA   PAIL
ROUTE   TOOL   ELBA
CANIGETAWITNESS
STEPONIT   BRAVES
      VAC   JAYLENO
COURIC   SOBS
LARIAT   WHATSNEW
OHNO   MAN   HIDE
PUSSYCAT   SMOKED
      IOUS   QUEENS
ISRAELI   GUS
OTELLO   DOASISAY
WOULDNTITBENICE
ALPO   EACH   LORNA
NEST   LIES   SNEER
```

It's a Piece of... (pages 6-7)

```
ERAS   PORT   STINT
TOFU   OREO   CANOE
COALMINER   RIFLE
   FRUITOFTHELOOM
         GIT   AAS
INSANE   NORM   CAM
PANFORGOLD   ERGO
ADORN   ANA   FLOAT
NERO   SPONGEBATH
ART   BOSS   AWAKES
      FLO   DRE
RICEUNIVERSITY
ELATE   TIMETRIAL
PIKES   CLOT   OLLA
SEEDY   HENS   NEED
```

Water Ya Expect (pages 8-9)

```
OMEN   SLOT   ATSEA
DALI   LILI   TWEED
EXEC   ITEM   TICKS
RIVERPHOENIX
      GIBE   FELTTIP
DROOPY   ELIA   ONO
EERIE   PAIL   SOLO
CHANNELSELECTOR
KING   LAYS   NAIVE
ERG   EDNA   CORNER
DEEPSET   SALE
      STRAITJACKET
OMAHA   IDIO   RAVE
BEGAT   NELL   OLIN
INAWE   SATE   WELT
```

Mish-Mash (pages 10-11)

```
FRITTATA   WALESA
RENOWNED   ONELEG
ESPRESSO   ANDEAN
STAREAT   EDU   CLU
CORED   TOT   MATTS
ANT   CRUNCH   MRED
      DOUBT   OPPOSE
CHORALE   CHIANTI
REPUTE   NOUNS
OMEN   SCHEME   LAB
SANKA   SLR   APACE
STA   NBA   CAPRICE
BIRDIE   SIPPYCUP
ATEASE   TOOLCASE
READER   UNPEELED
```

It's Good to Be the Queen (pages 12-13)

```
PIAF   RUIN   CCR
INTL   ESAU   RAE
CATEBLANCHETT
      EAR   SLATER
ASS   IMP   ENERO
BETTEDAVIS
SASH   LOA   ETON
      EMILYBLUNT
COSMO   OAR   NOH
ISLAND   IDI
GLENDAJACKSON
AID   ADAM   NIKE
RNS   YAMS   YADA
```

Clothing Alterations (pages 14-15)

```
LEAF   CST   EPEE
EARL   ATA   URNS
ERGO   REDCROSS
SPORTSTACO
      AYE   SPAWN
ARF   PASS   OBEY
BALLETRIPPLES
ISEE   SODA   EKE
THEFT   ETC
      TRACKHOSES
MARIACHI   VAYA
MIKE   TAC   EVER
EROS   IRK   REDD
```

ANSWERS

```
S T I N K   G A L E   B A R S
A R N I E   A B I T   U R A L
G A R T E R B E L T   L I N E
A Y E   P O O L   A L L E G E
      C M O N     A S S E T
R A N O U T   P R O S E
A L A R M   G R E A T S E A L
P U P A   P R I N T   S A L E
S M A L L T I M E   B I S O N
      G U S T O   B O O T E D
C R E A K     T O W N
H O T B E D   S O I L   T E A
E L A L   R A T T L E T R A P
E L I E   A R I A   R O U S E
P O L S   G I R L   S T E E D
```

```
S H A N G H A I   A L A S K A
N I N E P I N S   C E L T I C
E N T R A C T E   S T E R E O
E D I T S   E E N   T R I L L
R O C S   P R Y O R   T C B Y
S O S   I D I O T I C   T A T
      A N J O U   V A R E S E
S A N D B A R   A U R O R A S
I N A J A M   A R L E N
D A S   D E G R E E S   T E T
E T T E   S I T A T   L U T H
T H I N K   L I C   B A R R E
R E E S E S   S O L O N G A S
I M S U R E   A D E L A I D E
P A T E N T   N E A T I D E A
```

```
A S S   L A E   P U T S O U T
L L C O O L J   A B O L I S H
L E A K A G E   N O R E L C O
B A L D F A C E D L I E
U Z I   S E T S A T   P A I D
T E A S   I C S   P S Y C H
      H E N N A   M E L E E S
B L O W N G L A S S A R T
T O U P E E   A R G O T
R O L L S   A T E   E M E R
E T U I   P L E A D S   A N I
      F L A T S C R E E N T V
R L S T I N E   O D D S A R E
C A T E R E R   D R A G N E T
A D D R E S S   E E N   A E S
```

```
N D A K   P I N T   S M U
A E R O   A F A R   A U F
S A L L Y R I D E   B L O
A D O N A I   A B B O T
      R S A   E A T I T
  J U A N I T A K R E P S
P A P P   A R D   C U L P
V I R G I N I A D A R E
C L E A N   A M A
  B A R K S   W R A P U P
F I R   J A N E T R E N O
O R E   E G O S   I S I S
O D D   T A R T   D O T E
```

```
    N T H   B W I   S T A B
A M A R A   T U R N   T O R E
R E S I N   I T I S   U R A L
A N T E D A T E S   K N O L L
P U S S Y F O O T I N G
    M R S   L O U   B A N
M A L T A   D E S C R I B E
O C E A N   T O T   K I L L S
L I O N S D E N   L A K E S
E D S   H E X   A P E
    S O F T S H O U L D E R
S T E E P   I N S I N U A T E
I R A N   A L A I   D I N N A
P E S O   T E R N   E S T A R
S E E R   O S E   R A E
```

```
    C E L   G E M   B R E A
S O S O   O V O   E A T S
I M P R O V E D   I N C H
B O N E S T R E N G T H
      N U S   S E E
F I Z Z   F T S   V I E
B L O O D C L O T T I N G
I L E   I O U   H A N G
      O E R   U T E
  I M M U N E S Y S T E M
I D E A   E Y E S I G H T
M O T H   A R I   D E U S
P L E A   S E T   E L D
```

ANSWERS

Backstory (pages 28-29)

T	K	T	S		S	S	T		R	E	P	O
A	W	E	E		T	I	A		L	O	B	O
H	A	R	E		I	G	U	E	S	S	S	O
J	I	M	M	Y	C	H	O	O				
		E	E	K		N	E	S	T	E	A	
A	G	O		L	T	D		S	I	G	N	
M	A	N	O	L	O	B	L	A	H	N	I	K
A	L	E	C		A	A	H		A	S	H	
J	E	S	T	E	R		D	A	B			
			T	O	R	Y	B	U	R	C	H	
G	L	E	E	C	L	U	B		S	H	O	E
M	A	R	S		O	S	U		T	E	R	R
A	X	E	L		S	E	G		A	A	A	S

I Don't Like Mondays (pages 34-35)

B	U	R	G		R	A	E		F	A	S	T
O	R	E	O		E	L	L		U	T	A	H
I	N	A	S	E	N	S	E		R	O	W	E
	R	O	E	D	O	C	T	R	I	N	E	
	A	B	U	G			T	R	Y			
A	F	A	T		B	O	S	E		E	S	T
A	R	C	H	B	U	T	T	E	R	F	L	Y
A	O	K		E	C	T	O		U	F	O	S
		O	A	K			S	N	U	B		
K	E	Y	B	U	S	I	N	E	S	S		
I	D	E	A		K	L	O	N	D	I	K	E
A	D	A	M		I	S	M		R	V	E	R
S	A	R	A		N	A	E		Y	E	G	G

On the Tree (pages 30-31)

B	L	O	G	S		A	C	E		B	O	W
B	E	R	R	A		N	O	R		E	R	A
C	O	N	A	N		G	L	I	T	T	E	R
	A	D	E		E	T	C	H				
T	A	M	S		E	L	S		A	S	P	S
I	R	E		D	E	S		A	N	T	I	C
T	I	N	S	E	L		W	R	E	A	T	H
L	E	T	H	E		C	A	T		R	A	M
E	L	S	A		M	A	Y		A	L	S	O
			L	O	I	N		E	L	I		
G	A	R	L	A	N	D		T	I	G	H	T
O	N	O		T	E	L		A	C	H	O	O
D	Y	E		H	O	E		L	E	T	G	O

Politically Correct (pages 36-37)

P	O	D		T	E	M	P		P	R	A	Y
J	A	R		O	D	I	E		I	O	W	A
S	K	A		P	U	R	P	L	E	C	O	W
	W	I	I			A	T	A	L	L		
P	I	N	A	C	O	L	A	D	A			
I	B	E	G		P	O	S	Y		N	A	G
C	I	A	O		A	R	C		M	O	N	A
S	S	R		D	R	N	O		E	A	T	S
		P	O	T	A	T	O	C	H	I	P	
E	M	B	E	R				V	H	S		
P	E	R	R	Y	C	O	M	O		A	A	A
E	G	O	S		H	A	R	I		R	P	M
E	A	S	E		A	R	I	D		K	E	Y

Bang For The Buck (pages 32-33)

B	B	S		K	E	G		C	U	R	S	E
L	O	U		A	D	O		A	B	O	U	T
O	E	R		F	I	T		M	O	A	N	S
B	R	E	A	K	T	H	E	B	A	N	K	
	B	L	A	H			M	R	T			
O	L	E	O		V	M	I		S	C	I	
H	I	T	T	H	E	J	A	C	K	P	O	T
M	P	S		A	W	S		N	A	Y	S	
	P	L	O		B	O	A	C				
	S	T	R	I	K	E	I	T	R	I	C	H
A	L	O	O	F		T	N	T		O	O	O
N	O	R	M	A		A	G	E		U	R	L
D	E	T	O	X		T	O	R		S	E	E

Ice Squad (pages 38-39)

S	A	M		M	O	A	T		A	C	M	E
P	I	E		O	L	L	A		L	A	O	S
I	S	L	A	N	D	E	R		O	P	I	E
C	L	O	U	D	S		C	H	I			
Y	E	N	T	A		S	E	N	A	T	O	R
		R	Y	D	E	R	S		A	D	O	
E	S	P	Y		O	W	L		S	L	E	W
S	E	E		S	L	E	E	P	Y			
P	A	N	T	H	E	R		A	R	A	B	S
	G	U	Y			B	R	I	L	L	O	
P	I	U	S		P	R	E	D	A	T	O	R
E	R	I	K		A	U	T	O		O	A	R
P	A	N	S		S	E	A	N		S	T	Y

Stanley Cup MVPs (pages 40-41)

```
H I T ■ B E E R ■ H E R B
O R R ■ A L L Y ■ O L I O
T K O ■ M I K E B O S S Y
■ ■ T A B ■ ■ ■ L E E K S
P A T R I C K R O Y ■ ■ ■
E R I C ■ L A I C ■ S H U
A L E S ■ A B A ■ P I U S
T O R ■ B R U T ■ A B L E
■ ■ ■ G U Y L A F L E U R
S P O O R ■ ■ ■ O E R ■ ■
K E N D R Y D E N ■ I N K
I S T O ■ E A S T ■ A C E
M O O T ■ A M P S ■ N O G
```

Computer Cinema (pages 46-47)

```
M A C ■ C A R ■ A L I T
I T O ■ L O B O ■ R I D E
N O R ■ A L E C ■ O M E N
■ M O R T A L K O M B A T
■ N O H ■ ■ E R A ■ ■ ■
A H A B ■ S A T E ■ M I A
F O R B I N P R O J E C T
T R Y ■ C O T Y ■ E D I E
■ ■ P E W ■ ■ T A I ■ ■
W E I R D S C I E N C E ■
O R B I ■ H A R D ■ I D E
R I E N ■ O H M S ■ N I P
N E X T ■ E N A ■ E T A
```

Online Ennui (pages 42-43)

```
C H A ■ T A L ■ ■ C U R
A I L ■ E L I A ■ C A S A
P R O G R A M S ■ U R E Y
A T E R R I B L E B O R E
■ ■ ■ A I N ■ A R A L ■ ■
C O U P ■ A N I ■ I R A
O N T H E I N T E R N E T
G E E ■ L S D ■ E A V E
■ N O L O ■ E S T ■ ■ ■
I S S T I L L B O R I N G
N U I T ■ D I S C O V E R
K I L O ■ E R E I ■ A M A
S T S ■ ■ A N O ■ N O B
```

At One's Bidding (pages 48-49)

```
R E S ■ A P A R T ■ A T M
E L K ■ C U R I O ■ W I I
F L I G H T C O M M A N D
■ M E E T S ■ ■ O R C A
A I M E D ■ ■ I N L E T S
P O E ■ M E C C A ■ ■ ■
P U R C H A S E O R D E R
■ ■ R E N T S ■ ■ E R E
G A L A X Y ■ ■ A S C A P
O D E S ■ ■ P A S E O ■
W I T H O U T C H A R G E
N E O ■ I N A N E ■ U P S
S U N ■ L O S E S ■ M A P
```

Step Lively (pages 44-45)

```
D E C A L ■ A L L ■ P E R
E L I S A ■ P E A ■ U R I
F L A T B R E A D ■ M I T
■ ■ R O A D ■ L O P E Z ■
E S C O R T ■ N E W S ■ ■
F A L S E T T O ■ L I C E
T K O ■ R A I N Y ■ R A Y
S I G N ■ N O S E C O N E
■ ■ G A P S ■ A L A N I S
O M E G A ■ I L L S ■ ■ ■
D A D ■ S H O E S T O R E
E M U ■ T U T ■ A R I E L
S A P ■ A B A ■ T O L L S
```

Music Fit for a King (pages 50-51)

```
B O O L A ■ B A T ■ J I G
U L C E R ■ O H O ■ A D O
R E H A B ■ R A P ■ C O D
L O O K I N G B A C K ■ ■
■ ■ ■ S T U ■ ■ Z O R R O
P G A ■ E D D A ■ D U A L
U N F O R G E T T A B L E
M A T S ■ E R A S ■ Y E S
P R E S S ■ ■ R U E ■ ■
■ R A M B L I N R O S E ■
W I T ■ U P A ■ A R M O R
A K A ■ R O C ■ M E N S A
R E X ■ F E E ■ I D I O T
```

ANSWERS

Monster Heads (pages 52-53)

```
ROD█AMUCK█BYE
FRI█TAHOE█LOX
DRAGONFLY█ODE
██MEL█IPECAC
TROLLEYCAR██
HEN█SAO█DRDRE
ADDS█TUG█SEED
ROSIN█NEO█FED
██GORGONZOLA
EIGHTH██BEG
MME█HYDRANGEA
MAR█OMENS█EGG
AXE█TENSE█ROO
```

Social Networking (pages 58-59)

```
EGGS█HUM█PHAT
LOOT█ANY█HUGE
SANE█ILO█OMEN
EDGE█RIP█BASS
███LINKEDIN█
EMO█SEE█RAITA
NOUGAT█PASTOR
TETRA█ARC█YET
█FACEBOOK█
SPIN█MIT█ALMS
HEED█ODE█ROOT
ISLE█TEC█MALE
NODE█EST█ANEW
```

Log-in Information (pages 54-55)

```
SIRS█DOS█SWAB
LOAN█ERA█HERO
ETNA█ANT█HAIL
WAIF█LEI█SAT
██USERNAME██
COT█TRY█SALES
HIATUS█STREAK
OLDEN█SHE█DRY
█PASSWORD█
BRO█HER█ROMP
ROLE█ORT█AREA
EPEE█EVE█FEAR
DESK█DEN█TONK
```

Mouthpieces (pages 60-61)

```
LTD█SHAD█COAT
BRA█PAPI█RULE
JAMBOREE█ATOP
█ACIDTONGUE
PRANK██GEODE
CALF█CALL█
STIFFUPPERLIP
█ORBS█IOWA
ASTRO█AGLOW
SWEETTOOTH█
WING█SPLITPEA
ANTI█PEEL█EGG
NESS█SCOT█ZOO
```

There Auto Be a Law (pages 56-57)

```
CARS█ACCEPTOR
OWEN█WELLTODO
MONO█ADULATED
BLOWAKISS██
██BENT█MYTH
STOGY█GETAWAY
HARASS█RANCID
ACCUSER█PEALE
GOAL█NAPE█
█PAPARAZZI
NARCOTIC█TOED
ONEONONE█ONTO
TAMPERER█MEAL
```

In Position (pages 62-63)

```
BUMPY█MAP█COT
ATARI█USE█OAK
LAYINGSIEGETO
KHAN█REFLEX█
██TRA█SNIPS
IVS█BIAS█ISAK
SITTINGPRETTY
ISAY█YORK█SHE
SALSA██IOU
█WORKON█NASA
STANDINGEIGHT
OUR█ODE█STOAT
SGT█RDS█PEGGY
```

Beat It! (pages 64-65)

```
S C R A M ■ A C R E A G E
A L O H A ■ P R E S L E Y
N O M A D ■ T A C T I L E
E S P ■ A M E B A ■ ■ ■ ■
R E S ■ M I S S P I G G Y
■ ■ M E L T ■ ■ B A N E ■
D E L U X E ■ C A M P U S
A G A R ■ M A U S ■ ■ ■ ■
W O N K A B A R S ■ M B A
■ ■ M A N E S ■ ■ O R R ■
B I T P A R T ■ I D I O T
A V I A T O R ■ E U R O S
M E S S I N A ■ S E E D Y
```

Positively Charged (pages 70-71)

```
P R O T O N S ■ G U L F S
E A R S H O T ■ U R I A H
A D I P O S E ■ A N T R E
S I N ■ H E A R ■ T E A ■
Y O G I B E R R A ■ L A T
■ ■ B I D ■ E N M E S H ■
A M B I T ■ ■ T O R T E ■
R E A S O N ■ S E A ■ ■ ■
U L T ■ H A P P E N I N G
G A S ■ O P A L ■ R E L ■
U N M A N ■ C A S S A V A
L I E G E ■ E S T A T E S
A N N O Y ■ R H Y M E R S
```

Just The Facts (pages 66-67)

```
M A A M ■ C O A T T A I L
A B L E ■ A N N O U N C E
N E O N ■ P R O M P T E D
E T T U B R U T E ■ ■ ■ ■
■ ■ ■ L A S H ■ S P A T ■
B R I B E ■ H E R O I N E
A I R I E R ■ R O U T E R
B L O O P E R ■ S P A W N
Y E N S ■ C O M E ■ ■ ■ ■
■ ■ C L O I S O N N E ■ ■
R E C L A I M S ■ D E A R
E T H E R N E T ■ D A M S
S C A T T E R S ■ S T E T
```

Let's Eat! (pages 72-73)

```
C H O W ■ A S P S ■ B I T
H U G H ■ U T A H ■ A R E
I S L E ■ D O R Y ■ T I N
C H E E S E I T ■ B E S T
■ ■ ■ I N C I S E ■ ■ ■ ■
W H E R E ■ S E A L O F F
H A R A S S ■ S L I D E R
O N E S T E P ■ S E E D Y
■ ■ ■ P A E L L A ■ ■ ■ ■
M A S S ■ K E I S T E R S
I R A ■ V I A L ■ O P E N
T E N ■ I N S T ■ M I N I
T A G ■ A G E S ■ S C O T
```

Raise a Glass (pages 68-69)

```
A L E S ■ C R I T I C A L
L O U T ■ R U M I N A T E
A C R E ■ A P P E N D E D
S H O T Z B E E R ■ ■ ■ ■
■ ■ ■ A S E A ■ M O S H ■
S T A R R ■ S C R U P L E
K A L I F S ■ H O T A I R
E L A P S E D ■ W E L T S
W E R E ■ D E A D ■ ■ ■ ■
■ ■ ■ C A N D Y C O R N ■
O R A T O R I O ■ A R E A
L O N E L I E R ■ R E A R
D E C L A S S E ■ B O D Y
```

Colleagues (pages 74-75)

```
D A F T ■ C A M P ■ M R T
O H I O ■ I S E E ■ O H O
S I L E N T P A R T N E R
■ ■ A H O Y ■ ■ ■ O K A Y
D E M O N ■ U S S R ■ ■ ■
A X E L ■ I N C A ■ G O P
T E N D E R C O M R A D E
A C T ■ V O L T ■ A S I S
■ ■ ■ G E N E ■ T Y P E O
O A H U ■ ■ ■ S A G E ■ ■
D R I N K I N G B U D D Y
O A F ■ G I F T ■ N A N O
R B I ■ B I C S ■ S L A M
```

ANSWERS

iSolve (pages 76-77)

I	P	A	D		G	R	A	N	D	P	A	S
N	I	N	E		R	E	S	E	A	R	C	H
D	A	T	E		E	P	H	E	M	E	R	A
I	N	O	R	D	E	R		R	E	V	E	T
E	O	N		O	D	O	R			E	A	T
			P	O	I		O	R	A	N	G	E
S	H	R	I	N	E		C	A	N	T	E	R
L	I	E	G	E	S		K	I	T			
A	T	M		T	O	Y	S		S	O	T	
S	T	A	T	S		U	R	E	T	H	R	A
H	I	T	H	E	R	T	O		H	O	A	X
E	T	C	E	T	E	R	A		A	N	T	E
R	E	H	E	A	T	E	D		W	E	E	D

Seasonal Theme (pages 82-83)

P	A	S	S			T	A	S	T	E
A	L	E	U	T		A	L	C	O	A
L	I	N	E	S		B	L	O	W	S
E	A	S	T	E	R	B	U	N	N	Y
S	S	E			H	E	R	E	S	
			C	L	Y	D	E			
	C	L	A	I	M			A	A	A
P	A	I	N	T	E	D	E	G	G	S
A	D	M	I	T		A	N	A	I	S
S	E	I	N	E		T	I	T	L	E
O	T	T	E	R			D	E	E	T

Sweet for the Sweet (pages 78-79)

S	N	O	C	A	P	S		R	E	C	U	R
C	O	R	A	C	L	E		I	N	A	N	E
A	D	A	P	T	E	R		V	E	R	S	E
L	E	T	S		D	A	T	E		I	N	N
P	S	E	U	D		P	A	R		B	A	A
			L	A	T	E	R		O	R	C	
G	A	I	E	T	Y		R	E	S	U	L	T
R	U	N		I	D	Y	L	L				
E	D	S		O	N	E		K	A	R	S	T
N	U	T		O	G	L	E		V	A	N	E
A	B	A	S	H		V	I	S	I	T	O	R
D	O	N	E	E		E	R	O	S	I	O	N
A	N	T	E	D		R	E	D	H	O	T	S

Female Finishers (pages 84-85)

T	I	E	R		O	H	M		S	N	I	T
O	K	R	A		M	A	R		H	E	R	O
M	E	R	M	A	I	D	S		A	W	A	Y
			M	I	T			J	H	S		
G	O	F	E	R		B	E	E	S	W	A	X
A	R	I	D		Z	I	P	S		O	W	E
S	I	R		B	E	G	E	T		M	A	N
P	B	S		O	B	O	E		Z	E	R	O
S	I	T	S	O	U	T		L	I	N	E	N
		L	I	T			P	A	N			
O	P	A	L		S	H	O	P	G	I	R	L
L	E	D	A		H	U	M		E	R	I	E
D	A	Y	S		Y	E	P		D	E	M	O

The Art of Flower Arranging (pages 80-81)

T	A	M	I		N	A	G		S	T	E	P
O	V	E	N		A	D	E		C	I	A	O
P	I	N	K	R	O	S	E		O	G	R	E
			Y	A	M			C	R	E	S	T
S	L	C		F	I	S	C	H	E	R		
L	E	A	S	T		T	R	I	P	L	E	S
I	N	R	I		W	A	Y		A	I	D	A
D	I	N	G	I	N	G		A	D	L	I	B
		A	N	S	W	E	R	S		Y	E	E
B	A	T	H	E			A	H	I			
E	R	I	E		L	A	V	E	N	D	E	R
A	M	O	R		A	G	E		D	O	L	E
T	Y	N	E		M	O	L		Y	E	L	P

Sexiest Man Alive (pages 86-87)

N	O	A	H		A	F	A	R		C	C	S
O	N	C	E		D	E	L	I		O	L	A
L	A	O	S		D	E	P	P		M	O	I
T	I	R	A	D	E		H	A	R	M	O	N
E	R	N		A	D	I	A		A	U	N	T
			M	O	S		E	S	T	E	S	
	M	C	C	O	N	A	U	G	H	E	Y	
C	R	O	O	N		A	N	G				
R	A	N	K		O	C	H	O		W	S	J
U	P	N	E	X	T		I	N	H	A	L	F
I	R	E		M	E	I	N		O	N	E	K
S	I	R		A	R	U	G		L	E	E	J
E	L	Y		S	I	D	E		A	S	T	R

ANSWERS

Heroines of History (pages 88-89)

P	E	Z		F	I	L	E		P	O	L	O
A	G	E		O	V	E	R		L	U	A	U
T	O	P		R	O	S	A	P	A	R	K	S
		P	E	E	R			O	N	S	E	T
	B	E	T	S	Y	R	O	S	S			
A	L	L	O	T		E	A	T		P	M	S
G	O	I	N		I	R	K		T	H	A	I
O	W	N		B	R	A		A	W	A	R	D
			J	O	A	N	O	F	A	R	C	
E	S	S	E	X			L	I	S	A		
S	A	L	L	Y	R	I	D	E		O	F	F
A	W	O	L		E	V	I	L		H	B	O
U	N	T	O		F	E	E	D		S	I	X

Supermodels (pages 90-91)

B	I	S		G	R	A	T	A		O	F	T
A	N	N		R	I	L	E	S		N	A	Y
N	A	O	M	I	C	A	M	P	B	E	L	L
A	P	R	O	P	O	S			E	A	S	E
N	I	K	E	S			S	E	L	L	E	R
A	L	E			G	O	P	R	O			
	E	L	A	I	N	E	I	R	W	I	N	
		C	O	U	R	T			C	U	T	
C	A	C	T	U	S			C	R	E	M	E
A	L	O	E			B	R	O	A	D	E	N
C	I	N	D	Y	C	R	A	W	F	O	R	D
H	E	E		O	S	A	G	E		W	I	T
E	N	S		M	I	N	E	R		N	C	O

Lipstick (pages 92-93)

A	S	I	A		C	G	I		M	A	M	A
G	U	R	U		O	A	K		U	L	U	S
E	V	E	R	E	M	B	E	L	L	I	S	H
			O	A	F			A	T	T	H	E
C	H	E	R	R	Y	L	I	C	I	O	U	S
R	U	R	A	L		E	D	Y				
Y	E	A	S		B	E	A		S	E	A	L
			L	I	Z		A	H	E	A	D	
T	R	O	P	I	C	A	L	C	O	R	A	L
H	I	R	A	M			Y	E	W			
R	A	S	P	B	E	R	R	Y	B	I	T	E
E	L	E	A		D	O	I		I	C	E	D
E	S	A	S		S	E	C		Z	U	L	U

Parent Company (pages 94-95)

I	S	L		T	K	O	S		Z	E	D	S
B	E	E		R	U	T	H		I	M	E	T
I	R	E	M	E	M	B	E	R	M	A	M	A
S	U	Z	I	E	Q		M	E	A	N	E	R
	M	A	Y		U	M	P	S		A	T	V
			A	P	A	R		E	S	T	E	E
	N	I	G	H	T	M	O	T	H	E	R	
S	O	N	I	A		O	R	S	O			
E	T	C		S	U	M	P		W	O	W	
A	D	O	B	E	S		H	Y	E	N	A	S
M	O	M	M	I	E	D	E	A	R	E	S	T
A	N	E	W		U	N	U	M		A	T	E
N	E	S	S		P	A	S	S		L	E	T

Songs from the Heart (pages 96-97)

D	O	H			E	L	F		A	F	A	R
A	X	E	D		X	I	I		P	O	R	E
T	E	A	R	O	P	E	N		P	U	F	F
A	N	D	I	L	O	V	E	H	E	R		
			L	E	S			E	A	S	E	L
	A	L	L	O	U	T	O	F	L	O	V	E
A	M	I			R	E	V			M	E	G
L	O	V	E	M	E	T	E	N	D	E	R	
A	R	E	N	A			R	O	O			
		I	F	I	L	O	V	E	D	Y	O	U
U	N	T	O		T	A	I	L	G	A	T	E
R	A	U	L		D	R	E		E	N	R	Y
N	Y	P	D		S	S	W			G	A	S

Memorable Female Roles (pages 98-99)

T	E	C	H		J	A	B	S		K	A	L
A	S	I	A		O	B	I	E		N	R	A
B	L	A	N	C	H	E	D	U	B	O	I	S
			D	O	N	T		S	E	X	E	S
T	A	E	B	O			O	S	E			
I	L	S	A	L	U	N	D			M	E	M
S	L	A	G		L	E	O		B	A	R	E
A	S	U		N	O	R	M	A	R	A	E	
			B	A	A			A	N	G	S	T
P	I	L	A	F		S	A	Y	S			
S	C	A	R	L	E	T	T	O	H	A	R	A
Y	E	T		A	T	O	M		E	V	E	L
D	E	E		T	A	P	S		E	A	T	S

ANSWERS

Whose Shoes? (pages 100-101)

At Least It's More Common in Men... (pages 106-107)

Hair Throughout the Decades (pages 102-103)

Anti-What? (pages 108-109)

Shop 'Til You Drop (pages 104-105)

Feets Don't Fail Me Now (pages 110-111)

ANSWERS

Double Your Pleasure (pages 112-113)

S	T	O	W		B	A	C		X	M	A	N
L	O	L	A		A	T	O		X	O	R	O
A	G	I	R	L	S	H	O	U	L	D	B	E
V	A	N		E	A	R	L	S		E	S	L
			S	O	L	O	I	S	T			
P	R	O	P		T	W	O		A	D	I	P
M	E	R	I	T				E	R	I	T	A
T	H	I	N	G	S		C	L	A	S	S	Y
S	E	E		I	N	T	R	A		G	A	S
	A	N	D	F	A	B	U	L	O	U	S	
O	T	T	O		P	O	D		U	S	N	A
F	E	E	T		U	N	E		S	T	A	N
A	D	D	S		P	E	R		T	S	P	S

Girl Talk (pages 118-119)

I	T	S		S	H	O	W		S	P	A	Z
M	I	A		H	U	N	H		H	A	R	E
S	E	X		A	R	T	I		T	R	E	K
	C	H	A	R	L	O	T	T	E	R	A	E
S	L	O	M	O		E	A	T				
M	I	R	A	N	D	A	R	U	L	E		
L	P	N		E	R	A		N	N	E		
	S	A	M	A	N	T	H	A	F	O	X	
			O	R	D		U	S	E	T	O	
C	A	R	R	I	E	F	I	S	H	E	R	
E	X	I	T		N	O	S	H		B	E	A
O	L	L	A		D	I	E	U		L	A	D
S	E	E	S		S	E	E	P		E	L	O

Girls' Night Out (pages 114-115)

L	O	C	H	S		K	F	C		T	A	R
U	H	A	U	L		N	A	H		E	N	O
C	O	S	M	O	P	O	L	I	T	A	N	S
A	H	A	B		A	X	L		A	L	A	S
			U	P	I			R	E	E	S	E
M	A	R	G	A	R	I	T	A		O	T	T
A	B	E		R	U	M	O	R		N	E	T
L	E	A		A	P	P	L	E	T	I	N	I
A	T	R	A	S			I	R	A			
I	M	A	M		S	P	F		K	N	I	T
S	E	X	O	N	T	H	E	B	E	A	C	H
E	N	L		O	L	E		A	I	M	E	E
S	T	E		W	O	W		S	T	E	R	N

Womens' Firsts in Sports (pages 120-121)

T	E	C	H		T	A	L	K		T	N	T
W	A	R	E		A	L	A	N		A	I	R
O	R	E	S		P	I	C	O		B	A	Y
A	L	T	H	E	A	G	I	B	S	O	N	
	S	E	E	P	S			S	T	U	T	Z
			I	B	A	R		A	L	I	A	
D	A	N	I	C	A	P	A	T	R	I	C	K
A	R	E	A		R	O	P	Y				
M	A	G	M	A			S	R	T	A	S	
	B	A	B	E	Z	A	H	A	R	I	A	S
B	I	T		R	O	V	E		O	K	I	E
I	C	E		I	L	I	E		V	E	N	T
D	A	D		E	A	S	T		E	N	T	S

Poet's Muse (pages 116-117)

T	H	I	S		C	B	E	R		B	B	Q
R	U	N	T		A	L	E	C		E	E	E
A	M	S	O		P	U	R	R		N	E	D
M	O	U	L	I	N	R	O	U	G	E		
P	R	M	A	N			M	A	L	T	S	
			F	I	R	S	T	B	L	U	S	H
J	I	G		E	R	A		X	O	O		
O	C	E	A	N	L	I	N	E	R			
G	E	T	M	E			M	O	P	E	S	
	A	P	P	L	E	P	O	L	I	S	H	
M	A	J		H	A	T	E		A	P	S	O
E	X	O		E	Z	R	A		N	E	A	T
D	E	B		W	E	E	K		D	R	Y	S

Aim Higher (pages 122-123)

C	H	E	W		M	T	S			T	O	M
A	E	R	O		M	O	N		L	O	B	E
T	H	E	M	A	M	B	O		A	M	E	N
			E	M	M	E		T	C	B	Y	
M	I	N	N	Y		E	W	O	K			
A	N	E	W		S	Q	U	E	A	K	B	Y
U	T	A	H		A	U	S		M	O	M	A
S	O	L	O	N	G	A	S		B	A	W	L
			S	E	A	L		R	I	N	S	E
	J	E	E	Z		W	H	A	T			
L	O	D	E		J	I	U	J	I	T	S	U
S	A	N	K		R	T	E		O	O	P	S
D	N	A		S	H	Y		N	O	A	H	

ANSWERS

Kitchen Confident (pages 124-125)

```
T S P   M P A A   H E N
M I S O   E A R N   E L O
I N A G A R T E N   A L S
    R A C H A E L R A Y
R I S E S       T O T
O R T   E S O T E R I C
M A R T H A S T E W A R T
Y E A H S U R E     T E N
  P A H       F E E D S
J U L I A C H I L D
O R E   P A U L A D E E N
E S S   E R R S   Y E T I
L A S   D A T A   L A X
```

Cut Corners (pages 126-127)

```
C P A   A N E W   D A T
A R C   N O R I   O C H
B E E H I V E S T A T E
O G R E     K I D N A P
B O B D O L E   N E I G H
    P U M A   A C E D
  C R O P C I R C L E S
B L O C   E T C H
M I X E S   S H A G R U G
I M B A C K     T A P E
  B U N I N T H E O V E N
O R I   O U S T   E N T
N Y C   X E N A   R N S
```

Outfitted for Success (pages 128-129)

```
L O I N   J O G   S H A G
A N N O   U P C   Q E I I
P E R M   S A L   U R N S
D R E S S T H E P A R T
    G E O   F O R
E S P   N U T   L E A S H
S K I R T T H E I S S U E
T Y P E O   O A T   S E X
    B F F   T E A
  S H I F T W O R K E R S
J E E R   L A V   R I O T
E T A T   E W E   O R S O
W I T H   E A R   N E A P
```

Some Things for a Wedding Dress (pages 130-131)

```
H U H S   S C A M   F A B
B R I M   A U R A   E L O
O L D Y E L L E R   M O O
  A T T       T A U N T
N E W H A M P S H I R E
O R A   S O S P A D
M A Y O   T H O   E N Y A
  U P T A K E   O A T
  B O R R O W E D T I M E
H O W S O   I R S
E R N   B L U E T O O T H
E N E   E A S T   O M A R
L E D   D Y E S   P E G S
```

LBD (pages 132-133)

```
C U R L   I C U   G M E N
A R E A   N O N   R A V E
B A G U E T T E   A L I T
  L I T T L E D E V I L
  O R A   I K E
M A N E   P A T E   W H O
B L A C K E Y E D P E A S
A I L   I D E D   A L M S
  E S E   A L L
  D R E S S P A R A D E
J E E R   T I R E D O U T
O M N I   A T A   I N R E
T O T E   L A B   N E O N
```

Looking For Mr. Big (pages 134-135)

```
E N O S   L A I C   G M C
L E V Y   E U R O   R A H
I C E R   O D O R   A X E
  K R I S T I N D A V I S
O T T A W A   W E S T
K I A   A R E T H A
S E X A N D T H E C I T Y
  U N S E E N   N E E
J E A N   O R A T E S
C Y N T H I A N I X O N
R I D   O M N I   L U A U
E N O   O H N O   E C G S
W G N   T O O N   S H E A
```

ANSWERS

Woody Allen Films (pages 136-137)

```
A I D A   A B L E   M O B
H A I L   C O I L   A P E
A N N I E H A L L   N I A
    A X E     E T H E R
F I R S T   S O N I A
U S A   R E A R   E T N A
L E D   A L I C E   T E N
L E I F   S L A M   A R T
  O B O E S   B O N D S
V A D I M   M E L
I R A   I N T E R I O R S
S O Y   T O I L   V I A L
A D S   S T A T   E L M O
```

Desperate Housewives (pages 142-143)

```
W A S   A R C S   H O P
A C T   S O L O   R A V E
S H E R I D A N   A T O P
H E R O   M A N I C
  S N A R E   R U S H E D
    D E A L   R E E V E
B A H   C R O S S   R E B
A B U S E   S P E D
D E F E N D   A D E P T
  F E T E S   M A R C
R A M P   L O N G O R I A
E R A S   I D E A   I T S
D E N   S A W S   S E T
```

...But I Play One on TV (pages 138-139)

```
S A P   E D I T   B R A T
E R A   L A M E   R O L E
C L I F F H U X T A B L E
T O N E     S T U
    D A Y   B A C O N
S L O   P O D S   C A R E
H A W K E Y E P I E R C E
A R E A   O M A R   P A D
M A N T A   S E A
    L A B   G O A D
J E N N I F E R M E L F I
A R I A   A L O E   E R R
M E L T   R A N T   G O T
```

The Simpson Family (pages 144-145)

```
B E R E T   G U T   A B E
A G I L E   A S H   B A A
H O M E R   G E E   E R R
  V I M     M A T T
A N T E   O T H E R
L E A N   P R O   T O P
F O X   P I N   D O H
  N I A   E K E   P I L E
  R A T E S   L E E R
  L I F E   T I E
D I M   S A M   M A R G E
U S A   O L E   U S U A L
D A N   P I X   S E E P S
```

Miley Cyrus (pages 140-141)

```
S H O   F A L L   A P E
O U R   A L O E   A G E D
B R E A K O U T   L A N G
  S E T   A L I C E
A U D I S   C A M   N E D
A S E A   C O V E S
H A N N A H M O N T A N A
  S H E E N   I D O L
S E C   A R T   S C O R E
C E L E B   E E K
A R I D   B I L L Y R A Y
R I M S   O R A L   O L E
F E B   P A L S   W I N
```

Rock & Roll Hall of Famers (pages 146-147)

```
B A R B   D O C   B R A G
I D E A   I R A   L E N O
B O B S E G E R   O N T O
    A R I   L A N D E D
  S P L I T   A N D
P E A   C A R   T I A R A
C A L M   L E D   E L A L
S M E A R   M E D   O P T
    D O S   F A S T S
S T R O B E   E S P
L E O N   V A N H A L E N
I R O N   E L S   R I L E
P I T A   N E E   E D I T
```

ANSWERS

```
    T A P       M A R
  H O S E D   T R I A L
  F I S H E R   H I L T O N
  I R S   R I S E S   T O E
  N E E   V O N   R E S T
  E D S   G E L   A I D E S
        W I L D I N G
  S A L E S   I N N   S O P
  A C E D   M E L   T R I
  A T E   S A R A N   O D E
  B U R T O N   W A R N E R
    P E R M S   S N E E R
    D Y E       A D S
```

```
  A T A   B A A   C H I L E
  S U M   E N D   H O N O R
  I R E L A N D   I C A H N
  A B R A D E   F A U N A S
  G A I T S   C O N S E N T
  O N C E   B A R T
      A R G E N T I N A
          A T T Y   A S A P
  A S H A N T I   D I T C H
  C H A R G E   D E V O U R
  T A R O S   L I B E R I A
  I W E N T   P O R   I T S
  I N D I A   S R A   A Y E
```

```
  P E R P   O R E S   F E D
  O V E R   P O R K   U M A
  L O V E S T O R Y   N I T
        F I S T   S A N T A
  W O M E N   G A R Y
  A J A R   M E R I N G U E
  S A G   S T E E L   I R S
  P I N M O N E Y   C R A T
    O N U S   T U L L E
  A L L O F   D I E T
  L I I   F O O T L O O S E
  S P A   L I R A   F L A N
  O S S   E L A L   F E T E
```

```
  S P R I G   I R S   M R I
  H Y E N A   M E N   R E G
  A L E C S   A V O C A D O
  G E L A T O   R A Z O R
      S A N D L E R
  G R E E N T E A   A B B A
  A Y N   K I L N S   R E O
  B E E P   M A C K E R E L
      O N E Y E A R
  C O C O A   S T A P L E
  C A R R O T S   E S S E N
  U F O   M A P   R E A D D
  P S P   I C Y   S R T A S
```

```
  S T A R   V A S T   B O W
  H O M E   E L I E   R Y E
  A N E W   N I N E F O L D
  G I N A N D T O N I C
        R E E   E X C E L
  G O D M O T H E R   O R E
  A M O S   T E N   G L A D
  L E W   M A R G A R I T A
  A N N I E   R C A
      P E A R M A R T I N I
  G E O R G E I V   I N O N
  A P U   E N N E   F R E T
  G A R   R O A R   Y E L L
```

```
  T E S L A   M I G   B R A
  E S T O P   O A R   A O L
  C E L L P H O N E   L O P
      I R O N   T A L K S
  D O C T O R   C A R P
  B E H A V I O R   C O O P
  A N A   E Z R A S   I G O
  S O P S   O B T A I N E D
    S P A N   E L A T E S
  O N T A P   M R I S
  M O I   H O U S E K E Y S
  N R C   I N T   R E W E D
  I N K   D O T   I D E A S
```

ANSWERS

Inedible Edibles (pages 160-161)

```
O J S   H T M L   S T O W
R O E   O R E O   A R T Y
B E A N B A L L   R A T A
    L O O M     V A L E T
S N I T   P I E C H A R T
O B O E S   N A H
C A N D Y S T R I P E R S
      S H E   P A G E R
R O L L C A L L   U G L I
E I E I O     A X L E
E L I S   H A M R A D I O
S E C T   A B B A   O P T
E R A S   N O S Y   N O B
```

King of Cool (pages 166-167)

```
B U L B   R E M O   E F F
E S A U   I V A N   F L O
G E N T   V I C E   G E O
  R A C H E L R A C H E L
      H I T   O L E
U S O   D E M     L O N G
S I L V E R C H A L I C E
A N D I   G U S   L O T
    T A B   M T V
C O L O R O F M O N E Y
O B I   A L O E   E V E N
O O F   B A R R   C A T O
L E T   S S T S   K N I T
```

Gender Studies (pages 162-163)

```
A S T A   E B B   E W E S
S L A M   M E A   C O O P
S U S A N B A N T H O N Y
N E S T E R   G O O D
    I P O S   P I P E R
E G O   A I L S   N I L E
C A M I L L E P A G L I A
R I N D   S E L L   E A R
U T I C A   P A G E
    V A L E   T A M A R A
G L O R I A S T E I N E M
N E R D   C U E   L A D E
U T E S   H E R   E T O N
```

The Original (pages 168-169)

```
M A A M   T H O M   M P S
A M S O   H A I R   C R T
J O H N D I L L I N G E R
O R E G O N     P A T E
R E S O W   T H I E V E S
        C H E A P I E S
  M I C H A E L M A N N
S E C R E T E D
A S H A N T I   J U B A L
T H A W     S O N O R A
P U B L I C E N E M I E S
A G O   T A R A   E T A T
T A D   S W A P   T O S S
```

Black Eyed Peas (pages 164-165)

```
A L S O   C R U   R A T E
R E H A S H E S   E K E D
I G O T T A F E E L I N G
D O W   E S S   L A N K Y
    D E N T   H E X
A G O G   E L A N   H I T
N O W G E N E R A T I O N
T O N   V E N D   A B U T
    R E D   W A G E
A C T O R   P I C   R I O
C L A P Y O U R H A N D S
M A K E   F R E E B I E S
E Y E S   F E D   C A S A
```

American Gangster (pages 170-171)

```
E B B   S H A M   S C A R
V E E   C E L I   T A C O
E L F   A M A T   A N N A
  R U B I N C A R T E R
F A I R S     H I T
I B E G   S U E D   S T E
B O N E C O L L E C T O R
S Y D   E L A L   A R I A
    O R D     O R A L S
T R A I N I N G D A Y
S E W N   E Y E D   C O T
P E A K   R E N E   A D O
S K Y S   S T A R   T E M
```

ANSWERS

Our Fair Lady (pages 172-173)

R	H	O		F	A	A		C	H	O	S	E
I	A	N		U	R	L		O	O	H	E	D
M	R	T		N	B	A		A	W	N	E	D
	T	H	E	N	U	N	S	S	T	O	R	Y
		E	D	Y	S		I	T	O			
T	H	A	I			I	M	A		M	A	S
W	A	I	T	U	N	T	I	L	D	A	R	K
O	R	R		N	O	T			E	M	M	Y
			P	S	A		E	L	A	M		
R	O	M	A	N	H	O	L	I	D	A	Y	
A	N	E	R	A		V	I	M		M	A	A
I	T	R	I	P		U	Z	I		I	N	A
L	O	E	S	S		M	A	T		A	K	A

The Fresh Prince (pages 178-179)

S	N	U	G		N	I	M	H		L	A	W
K	O	N	A		O	K	A	Y		A	L	E
I	A	M	L	E	G	E	N	D		M	D	S
S	H	A	L	L			I	R	O	B	O	T
		N	I	M	S		C	A	N			
H	A	N	C	O	C	K			O	G	R	E
U	N	E		S	I	G	N	E		L	E	N
E	N	D	S			B	A	D	B	O	Y	S
			E	A	U		M	I	R	A		
P	O	U	N	D	S			F	E	T	E	S
R	A	P		H	A	P	P	Y	N	E	S	S
O	H	O		O	G	L	E		D	R	A	T
S	U	N		C	E	O	S		A	S	I	S

Impersonation Station (pages 174-175)

G	I	S	H		S	L	A	P		C	H	E
O	T	T	O		T	I	L	L		H	O	P
B	E	A	U		L	E	I	A		R	U	E
	M	R	S	D	O	U	B	T	F	I	R	E
			E	A	U		I	S	I	S		
A	P	O		L	I	V			S	T	E	P
T	H	E	F	I	S	H	E	R	K	I	N	G
A	I	D	A			S	U	E		E	T	A
		E	R	A	S		G	E	M			
J	A	K	O	B	T	H	E	L	I	A	R	
A	L	E		B	E	A	N		N	G	O	R
N	O	R		O	N	Z	E		D	E	A	D
E	E	K		T	O	Y	S		Y	E	N	S

Interruptions (pages 180-181)

F	I	G		J	A	W			B	A	T
I	D	O		O	R	E		E	L	I	
B	E	S	T	B	E	T		D	I	T	
	A	H	A					B	A	H	
			P	L	A	N		U	S	E	
		B	E	A	N	B	A	G			
A	S	I		S	T	A	R				
B	E	G					A	R	C		
B	I	B		B	A	R	B	E	L	L	
O	N	E		A	G	O		S	U	E	
T	E	N		D	E	W		T	E	D	

Hollywood Prom King (pages 176-177)

R	H	E	A		G	I	F	T		E	B	B
E	O	N	S		U	L	L	A		M	A	O
F	I	G	H	T	C	L	U	B		A	M	I
		A	L	E	C			D	I	B	S	
A	N	G	E	L	I	N	A	J	O	L	I	E
H	U	E	Y			A	V	O	N			
A	N	D		A	S	H	E	S		S	C	I
			E	T	T	U		S	U	R	F	
T	W	E	L	V	E	M	O	N	K	E	Y	S
H	A	L	F				T	A	I	L		
U	S	B		R	U	S	T	Y	R	Y	A	N
G	T	O		A	N	T	E		T	O	D	O
S	E	W		P	O	U	R		S	N	O	B

It's Spring! (pages 182-183)

	K	M	A	R	T		Q	T	I	P
T	A	I	P	E	I		U	R	N	S
A	R	R	I	V	E		I	O	T	A
N	A	E	S			U	T	U	R	N
	T	S	H	I	R	T		T	A	D
			D	E	A					
A	U	G		I	P	H	O	N	E	
C	N	O	T	E			P	A	R	S
O	D	O	R		T	H	E	O	R	Y
L	I	N	E		S	E	R	M	O	N
D	D	A	Y		E	M	A	I	L	

ANSWERS

It's Spring! (pages 184-185)

E	P	I	C	S		D	O	Z	E	D
T	R	I	A	L		U	N	I	T	E
C	O	I	L	O	F	M	E	T	A	L
				W	E	B				
E	L	L	A		D	E	A	L	E	R
L	E	A	P	F	O	R	W	A	R	D
F	E	S	T	E	R		E	X	E	S
			R	A	H					
W	A	T	E	R	S	O	U	R	C	E
A	T	I	M	E		O	N	I	O	N
D	O	N	U	T		T	O	G	O	D

Geography Riddles (pages 186-187)

A	M	S		E	G	G		S	A	M
T	O	W		L	E	O		L	I	E
O	N	E		F	L	O	R	I	D	A
M	A	D				E	D	E	N	
I	C	E		B	O	O	M			
C	O	N	N	E	C	T	I	C	U	T
			E	A	T	S		A	S	I
O	K	L	A				S	E	T	
G	E	O	R	G	I	A		I	D	A
R	D	S		A	N	N		N	U	N
E	S	T		S	K	Y		O	P	S

Uplifting Melodies (pages 188-189)

C	A	R	B		T	A	D	A		B	B	S
A	F	A	R		E	M	I	R		E	E	K
R	I	C	E	P	A	P	E	R		A	L	E
P	R	E	L	I	M		S	I	G	N	U	P
E	E	R		E	M	S		D	E	I	S	T
			I	T	A	L	O		N	E	H	I
E	L	E	V	A	T	O	R	M	U	S	I	C
Y	E	S	I		E	P	I	C	S			
E	A	T	E	R		S	E	C		P	R	O
S	P	A	D	E	D		N	O	S	H	O	W
O	T	T		D	I	R	T	Y	P	O	O	L
R	A	E		I	D	E	A		O	N	M	E
E	T	S		G	I	L	L		T	E	S	T

Compose Yourself (pages 190-191)

S	H	I	V		O	K	A	Y		C	A	W
L	O	N	I		F	A	L	A		A	P	E
A	P	E	X		F	L	O	W		B	O	B
B	I	Z	E	T	S	I	G	N	A	L		
			N	O	H			S	P	E	C	K
A	C	E		S	O	U	P		E	C	H	O
B	A	C	H	H	O	M	E	A	G	A	I	N
A	R	C	O		T	A	R	P		R	A	G
S	P	E	R	M			I	S	P			
		H	A	Y	D	N	G	O	S	E	E	K
P	L	O		B	R	I	E		A	R	L	O
J	A	M		A	N	T	E		L	I	L	O
S	O	O		D	O	E	S		M	E	E	K

Frozen Exile (pages 192-193)

S	H	A	G		A	T	R	A		P	S	S
T	O	R	O		I	R	A	S		A	T	O
I	N	E	A	R	N	E	S	T		N	O	R
L	E	A	P	A	T		O	N	A	I	R	
E	S	S	E	N		M	O	R	O	C	C	O
			D	R	A	G		S	H	A	W	
C	O	O	L	Y	O	U	R	H	E	E	L	S
A	C	N	E		B	R	E	A				
S	T	A	N	L	E	Y		D	I	E	G	O
C	A	D	D	Y		C	O	N	M	A	N	
A	N	I		S	E	T	O	N	F	I	R	E
D	E	M		O	L	E	G		U	L	N	A
E	S	E		L	I	D	S		N	E	I	L

MLB Records (pages 194-195)

M	A	R	K		L	A	M		W	I	N	S
A	L	O	E		O	N	E		A	R	E	A
H	O	M	E	R	U	N	S		F	A	W	N
	T	O	N	E			A	P	E			
			E	D	I	T		A	R	O	M	A
	B	A	S		S	O	A	R		P	E	R
H	I	T	T	I	N	G	S	T	R	E	A	K
A	D	O		S	T	A	T		A	N	T	
T	E	N	S	E		S	I	F	T			
			P	E	A		A	I	D	E		
B	A	B	A		S	H	U	T	O	U	T	S
A	L	A	N		H	E	S		N	A	N	A
H	I	T	S		Y	E	A		S	L	A	M

ANSWERS

Play Ball! (pages 196-197)

B	A	B	E		L	A	P		P	O	P	S
A	R	A	T		E	L	I		A	L	T	O
W	I	T	H		F	I	E	L	D	D	A	Y
L	A	M	E	N	T		D	A	D			
		O	L	E			D	E	P	O	T	
E	B	B		W	A	I	T		D	I	R	E
L	E	I		S	T	R	A	Y		T	E	E
M	E	L	T		M	E	R	E		C	O	N
S	T	E	R	N			A	S	H			
	E	A	R		S	H	A	P	E	S		
R	U	N	A	B	O	U	T		L	I	V	E
U	N	I	T		A	S	A		A	P	E	X
M	O	P	S		R	A	Y		D	E	N	Y

Whip It! (pages 198-199)

A	I	R		S	C	O	W		S	C	U	M
P	I	A		A	B	B	Y		K	A	N	E
E	I	N	S	T	E	I	N		U	R	S	A
		K	A	R	E	N	A	L	L	E	N	
M	U	L	A	N			C	L	O	T		
A	T	I	T		F	O	O	D				
K	A	T	E	B	L	A	N	C	H	E	T	T
			E	Y	R	E		O	R	E	O	
O	R	B	S			O	L	A	N	D		
S	H	O	R	T	R	O	U	N	D			
P	A	S	O		O	B	S	E	S	S	E	D
A	R	I	D		Y	O	D	A		I	V	Y
M	A	N	Y		S	E	A	L		D	E	E

In the Lead (pages 200-201)

A	P	A	R	T		S	I	N		D	A	Y
S	A	V	O	R		H	O	E		I	R	A
P	R	E	S	I	D	E	N	T		R	E	N
S	T	R	I	P	E	D		T	W	E	A	K
			E	L	M		B	L	O	C		
L	U	C	R	E		S	C	E	N	T	E	D
A	S	H			D	A	D			O	R	R
S	E	A	P	O	R	T		S	P	R	A	Y
		I	O	U	S		F	L	O			
L	O	R	E	N		K	E	E	N	I	N	G
O	H	M		C	O	N	D	U	C	T	O	R
V	I	A		E	W	E		T	H	O	S	E
E	O	N			S	E	W		H	O	N	E	Y

The Crossword Without a Theme (pages 202-203)

A	J	A	R		R	O	E		H	A	R	P
V	I	T	A	M	I	N	D		O	V	E	R
O	N	T	H	E	P	L	U	S	S	I	D	E
W	X	Y		G	U	Y		A	E	S	O	P
			Z	A	P		E	M	S			
J	A	P	E			C	A	B		A	H	A
F	R	E	N	C	H	Q	U	A	R	T	E	R
K	E	G		Z	E	D			N	E	W	T
			V	E	X		V	W	S			
A	Z	T	E	C		D	O	E		L	O	S
W	E	I	G	H	E	D	I	N	W	I	T	H
E	T	N	A		B	A	C	T	E	R	I	A
S	A	Y	S		B	Y	E		B	A	S	H

Current Events (pages 204-205)

A	N	I	M	E		J	I	B		E	P	A
P	E	D	A	L		U	F	O		T	A	C
B	A	I	T	A	N	D	S	W	I	T	C	H
S	P	O	U	T	E	D		D	U	T	Y	
		T	R	E	X		S	A	O			
B	A	B	E		T	I	K	I		O	K	S
C	L	O	S	E	D	C	I	R	C	U	I	T
D	A	X		T	A	U	T		A	T	T	Y
		W	A	Y		T	I	N	T			
B	L	A	H		R	E	D	T	A	P	E	
R	E	C	O	R	D	B	R	E	A	K	E	R
O	A	T		U	N	I		S	T	E	E	R
S	K	I		M	A	S		T	A	S	K	S

That's a Hot One (pages 206-207)

J	A	P	E		E	C	C	E		M	A	X
A	S	E	A		R	O	A	R		A	B	E
M	I	C	R	O	W	A	V	E	O	V	E	N
B	A	K	E	L	I	T	E		U	S	D	A
		E	D	E	N		M	E	G			
N	E	D			P	A	T	H	W	A	Y	
F	R	A	N	K	L	I	N	S	T	O	V	E
L	A	T	E	F	E	E		R	A	W		
		A	C	T		D	V	D	S			
O	B	I	T		I	C	E	C	R	E	A	M
T	O	P	O	F	T	H	E	R	A	N	G	E
T	W	O		E	G	A	D		M	E	E	T
O	L	D		W	O	W	S		A	D	D	S

ANSWERS

Crossword (pages 208-209)

Part of a Rainbow (pages 212-213)

This Is the Day (pages 210-211)

Appreciation (pages 214-215)

Number One at the Box Office
(pages 216-217)

Playing the Role of Heroes
(pages 220-221)

Not Just a Department Store Santa
(pages 218-219)

The Apatow Empire (pages 222-223)

ANSWERS

"Lucy, I'm Home!" (pages 224-225)

```
CUBA   SAP   CBS
OPED   ADE   OOH
ITSA   STAR  AWE
TOOMANYGIRLS
    BARELY
AMA  EFS     ETAT
BABALU   DESILU
SEAL   TIE   MAX
    EASYGO
  RICKYRICARDO
JON  IRAN  HOOK
ACT  SIN   AMIE
RKO  SAT   BAND
```

"She Did it the Hard Way" (pages 228-229)

```
AMAT  DDT   AMMO
MACHFIVE  WEEK
CATEREDAFFAIR
   SET    AUDRA
BASTE  HALL
ASIA  CONS  DAG
CHARLOTTEVALE
HEM  IVES   IRON
   KTEL  MCKEE
ADIEU   COT
JOHNPAULJONES
OMAN  THEOREMS
BODY  EFF   YOUR
```

Footsteps (pages 226-227)

```
DANG  BBS   SEWN
ELON  AAH   HARE
WAROFTHEROSES
   COT    OWENS
DOLCE  TRAY
AMAH  LEES   SSE
BASICINSTINCT
ANT  ALOT   DEAR
   TSAR   SCENE
SHOUT   AMA
PERFECTMURDER
ERST  ORE   DRAY
WOOS  PAX   SERE
```

From Circus to Star (pages 230-231)

```
ALF  ALARM   PIP
HOI  MANIA   ILL
SUSPICION   ZIA
   HATE   DOZEN
PENNYSERENADE
AGES   TALE
TOT  SCHWA   NAB
   SWAY    LOBO
HISGIRLFRIDAY
ODETS   OHMS
PAR  HOUSEBOAT
PHI  ERNST   FBI
YON  SKEET   FEE
```

ANSWERS

BBC MD (pages 232-233)

A Successful Smile (pages 234-235)